Afteı

CW01480937

a novel by

Pelham McMahon
©2015

To Kathryn
with love from Anne
xxx

(Pre-edited copy – couple of
mistakes – tooth power should
read 'powder'. and the
'a' is missing I appreciate but
otherwise it is readeable.
Do miss you at Christ Church but
hope you are happy and well)

The right of Pelham McMahon to be identified as the author of this work has been asserted by her in accordance with sections 77 and 78 of the Copyright, Designs and Patents Act, 1988.

ISBN 13: 978-1508886525

ISBN 10: 1508886520.

For full listings of work by this author and playwright please consult the Web Page

pelhammcmahon.co.uk

Cover Photography by Sam Skull
e. mail sam.skull@hotmail.com

See - pelhammcmahon.co.uk
for the full list of works by Pelham McMahon, including
Platinum Ten
The DCI Teasdale Books
An Actors Place
And various dramas available for production.

Author's Comment.

I felt driven to publish this book even though I could not afford my usual proof reader, Julia Gibbs. If you find a mistake, don't blame her. Instead, please just be kind to this old dyslexic writer, who is racing against the clock to see her works in print, a dream I have held for the whole of my life.

In writing 'Aftermath' I am letting go of some of my childhood sorrows, while acknowledging some of the truths about Liverpool, which I have discovered. People no longer speak of the War time pain endured by this City, which has now been my home for 25 years. This modern historical novel is also dedicated to my family and friends, with a special mention of the Monk family. I frequently saw their son Nathan chatting with his own Grandmother, Vivien, a church friend of mine, and the very charming cameo of their relationship inspired me to create the character and story of Freddie Woods and his great-aunt.

Please, don't ask me where my other ideas came from, some of the historical events in the novel relate to real happenings, but in order to curtail the number of characters in the storyline several threads have been amalgamated and names have been changed.

Special thanks are given to CreateSpace for their wonderful free service and to Amazon for selling my books: to Dragon Naturally Speaking, the dictation software used in the writing of this volume, to the BDA [The British Dyslexic Ass.] for all their supportive work. To ALLi, the Alliance of Independent Authors for advice and guidance.

And finally I must say thanks to Sam Skull for the brilliant cover photo taken outside St Nicholas Church and the Liver Building.

Contents.

Chapter 1

How Freddie Woods gets to University.

First, I must tell you that, if and when I reach old age, I might still be wondering why I had opted to read history at University: any university, never mind Liverpool.

Many youthful choices are the stuff of dreams, the nightmare of parents, the disappointment of teachers, and the despair of hopeful employers. If education is meant to progress society towards ever greater heights of valuable employment, health, governance, justice, and peace on earth between all men, why do we pay so little attention to the product that is ejected from the hallowed halls of childhood academia?

The memory of my sixth form career's master Mr Williams almost shouting at me, will probably still leave me blushing with shame at my rebellious and childish indecisiveness, fifty years from now, never mind that particular week as I struggled to make a decision! Where to next?

As with all unwilling sixth formers at the well-named Albert Einstein Sixth Form Academy, I had long ago dispensed with anything resembling school uniform, except for a loosely knotted Academy tie, which allowed for the top two buttons of my shirt to hang open in what I regarded as a casual sexy invitation to the girls, but don't worry, there was hardly a single manly hair on my chest.

I remember I would stand propped up against the proverbial bike shed, in my habitual slouching, especially when wearing my best torn Levi jeans and well-worn sheep-skin stylish bomber jacket; the latter an amazing antique remnant from the 40's, bought for a tenner at a Cancer Research Charity Shop.

When my mother said I reminded her of James Dean, I embarked upon an orgy of DVD watching, beginning with *Rebel without a Cause*. I then devoured *East of Eden* and *Giant* with a passion that I still remember as my teenage hormonal period. I countered the spotty face with excessive cleanliness and attention to my hairstyle and clothes; hence I found sufficient female adoration to pacify my rapidly developing confidence when chatting up members of the opposite sex. Happy memories of teenage years: but girls aside, there I was enduring Mr Williams and the supposed one sided discussion upon my future career.

As per usual, I had my thumbs hooked into my Levi jeans pockets and the James Dean quiff of my hair uncombed. I knew I was annoying Old Williams, I could see the anger boiling up from his neck and right into his now crimson coloured cheeks. Even his ears looked fit to explode. I felt my power, and I revelled in it. I sunk deeper into my slouching pose and waited. James Dean would have been proud of me.

"Freddie Woods, stop dithering about, you have to put something down on the UCAS form and to be honest the only subject where you have had consistent high marks has been, history. So put it down, check out the universities; go and have a good look, get yourself known; discuss with your other teachers: but my advice is, do a year of history at any University daft enough to accommodate a lazy lump, such as yourself."

He paused, his brow glistening with sweat as he prepared the next stage of his onslaught. I waited in silence. I had avoided the man for months and doubted he knew anything about me, beyond the illegible comments from my year master. Unsure of how effective my silence was, I nevertheless believed that not giving him any ammunition would be the safest option.

"Then if you don't like it; you will at least have some idea as to which subject you could swap with in your second year, when lecturers will be desperate to avoid second year fall-off and knowing you, young man, they would probably be glad to get rid of you to something innocuous: media studies or the military!"

I looked at him with evident puzzlement. he noticed and added, "Oh yes, it won't hurt you, but it will at least get you into university, somewhere, anywhere, because if you don't, you will find yourself no more than a statistic in a national survey of youth unemployment, and living on the dole, at home with your parents, until you are thirty-five, or squatting in some backwater off the Mile End Road. Have you any idea where you might want to go?

So he had read The Times survey on 'Youth unemployment and problems with the Housing Market!' He sounded more and more like my parents and my 6th form tutor.

Then to my annoyance, I was forced to remind myself that there were the examples of efficiency from my more energetic peers. Yes, every one of my friends in the sixth form had made their decisions, filled in the wretched documents and had sent in their UCAS forms several days ago, some even as far back as a month ago.

I had no idea what to do with my life, sixteen plus years lived in a nowhere place named Vange, and you may well ask, "Who has ever heard of Vange?"

Unless you know Basildon, you won't know Vange: that is unless you are familiar with its two watering holes, The Old Barge Inn or its rival, The Five Bells. Originally Vange was just a small two pub village that became sucked into the post-war new town, named Basildon. To which your listener would say, "Basildon?" and you would reply, "Basildon in Essex!"

People always said it thus; 'Basildon in Essex' as if aware that the rest of the world had no idea where the place was or what it signified, and if you just said Basildon, they immediately thought of the superior notepaper known as Basildon Bond, which as far as I am aware, has nothing to do with the area in which I was born and bred.

Yes, I am he, Frederick Woods; from a nowhere place preparing himself for the inevitable onslaught from his parents, when he relays to them the Career master's low opinion of his academic abilities.

Delay the moment, imagine the scenario, no don't imagine it, try and forget it and slip down to the pub with your mates! Is this what they mean by a split personality?

Friday Pub night came and went, and all day Saturday I avoided every opportunity to discuss the matter with my parents, the amazing surgeon the Mr Raymond Woods and his wife, Staff Nurse Sally Woods. They had married late, so Mum explained, hence I was never expected: my personal opinion is that they were old before their time, being dedicated career people in the NHS and both complete workaholics! Their service of mankind had even extended to the support of the military. Both had volunteered and served at Camp Bastion Hospital.

There would be no point in claiming any form of child neglect during their many and varied absences from my life: a perfectly wonderful live-in Nanny had attended to my every need until I was sixteen years of age. The trouble began when she was retired on that momentous birthday. Legally I was considered mature enough to care for myself. Reality bit the hand that fed it; with Nanny gone the parents took it in turns to at least oversee my activities. Father took early retirement from the NHS and only did private work to suit him, while mother went on something called 'The Bank!' An agency run for someone's benefit: I never understood anything about it. My policy at home was to be as invisible as possible. It didn't work because they ran our home as a military establishment.

Can you hear them?

'Freddie, get up, now, that's an order.'
'Freddie, you are late.'
'Freddie, clean your room now.'
'Freddie, get off the phone.'

'Polish your shoes, young man.'

'Stop slouching!'

'Stand up straight!'

'What time do you call this?'

'No, Freddie you may not go to Amsterdam with   the rugby team!'

I think you get my drift!

If by any chance you listened to them, you would believe that they suffered their entire lives wondering what to do with their layabout offspring. Their only child, coming up to seventeen and more interested in pop music and computer games, was evidently a complete stranger to them.

Forced into it by the passage of time, I eventually told my parents what Mr Williams had said. As usual I chose the wrong time and the wrong place, because that day we had a house full of family for Sunday dinner and I unwisely believed I was cushioned, protected even, by the presence of four doting Grandparents and some of the younger members of the Houghton - Woods clan. Yes, the entire weight of family history sat around that dinner table listening to me give voice to Mr Williams's comments on my future prospects.

We were eating a wonderful Sunday lunch as English as roast beef and Yorkshire pudding could ever be; only it was minced beef, because of the presence of the maternal Grandparents, and as always Mother felt sorry for her father's difficulties with his false teeth: if he had to eat his beef minced, so did the rest of us! Why couldn't he just have his two slices minced and the rest of us enjoy cutting up chunks of the chewable splendour that is the ancient tradition of a British Sunday dinner? No, my mother had extraordinary ideas about inclusiveness. To this day I still dispute with her on her attitude to people's individuality. I believed I have a right to be myself, she believed I did not have any such right. Neither did her father, she just had to embarrass him by making his poor unfortunate teeth ruin all our dinners. I promise you, I felt sorry for the old man.

'Family is family, Freddie, and you will toe the line or get out.' She had always said that whenever I moaned about Sunday dinners with relatives crowding around our large mahogany dining table, and dominating the conversation.

She was quite tough my mother, and on that Sunday I rebelliously slopped my food in its gravy as I repeated my news,

"Well, Mr Williams said, History!"

Thus it was that I had chosen the wrong moment, for as I said, that day we were sitting at the dinner table surrounded by a gaggle of relatives from both sides of the family, plus four of my cousins, all of whom had been summoned to aid the discussion of my future.

Drawing no immediate reaction from my father, I yet again announced, "Mr Williams says, History!'

They all looked at me in silence; I looked at father who was gradually going puce, until unable to contain his rage, he began shouting at me in the classic parental response to a wayward son, but I sat in stony silence throughout his rant. Predictably, my silence only increased his anger.

'History?' He roared with all the passion of a Dickensian bully.

I could just as easily have said, 'the sex life of a praying mantis' or 'how to improve your income by robbing a bank.' He wasn't listening to me: as he screamed at me again, he seemed unaware of everyone else in the room.

'History?' The repetition was typical of my father; as if by saying it twice he could hammer home his disgust. I know I was destroying his dream; that his only son was to follow him into the medical profession, or second best, into the military in the footsteps of a glorious and affectionately remembered Great-Grandfather. I had lived all my youthful life admiring the gleaming medals as earned by the many members of all branches of my ancestors: we were a family proud of our military and medical background, and at that moment in time I knew that my father felt that I had just slapped his face with a cold flannel, or should that be a cold uncooked piece of fish, cod perhaps?

Then my maternal Grandparents joined in the debate, but they were more helpful and offered up the suggestion that, "You are welcome to live with us if you want to go to London University: if you want cheap lodgings!" and then

Grandma added, "I could cook for you." Living on Grandma's minced lamb stew bulked up with pearl barley put an end to that idea. I loved her, but her stews! And Grandad's teeth!

Mother was white faced, but she nudged Matt, my cousin, whose father and Grandfather had both been in the RAF, and as if on cue he smiled at her and said,

'Don't fret, Auntie, I'll have a chat with him.' She nodded as in agreement and even before I had finished eating my apple pie and custard, he hauled me to my feet before walking, no, marching me down to the bottom of the garden; where we were eventually joined by my cousins, Robert, Frankie and Angela.

I look back with gratitude for the time we spent together that day. They had been invited by Mum: did she know I would listen to them rather than to my father? Mum liked Matthew, at twenty five a banker and an ardent weekend TA man. Then there was Robert an IT manager, and also Frankie, two years older than me and already in his second year at RADA and his twin, Angela who was at the Royal School of Music. All four of *my cousins listen to my grievances and I listened to them, as they argued both sides, for and against going to university. They advised me to choose quickly and get in with a Fresher's crowd, rent a house or live in Student Halls of Residence: anything but don't live with relatives. Now that was a piece of advice I could readily accept.*

If you lived in an extended family where everyone knows your business, where all your Aunts and Uncles seem to be forever questioning, prying and wanting to know who you are seeing, what you are doing, and what you want to do when you leave college: I'm certain you quickly realize the pressure that they put me under, and will understand that the thought of being in a remote place, living with young people of my own age, and unconcerned if I have to live on baked beans every day, that regardless of good or evil: that was what I wanted to do and would do, if they would only get off my back!

That was then, this is now: I have grown up so that nowadays, I don't despise my elderly relatives, they just occasionally irritate me: chiefly because I sensed then and now, it was all a game of one–up–man–ship as each tried to present their offspring as the best in the pack.

Understandable, I suppose: Matthew, older and wiser and working for good money in an Investment Bank in Central London, was foisted with the misfortune of being the trail blazer for the rest of us, but I liked him every bit as much as I enjoyed Rob's company. Now, Rob had a job in 'Computers' and sometimes I thought I might like such a career because he seemed to live and breathe the games I loved. My other cousins, from my mother's side of the family; Frankie, he was talented, as was his twin, Angela. One was destined for the National Theatre or Hollywood, the other for Wigmore Hall, and all points proverbial for a genius of a concert pianist.

But, what of my personal talents! I could kick a football and had just been labelled as good at history, and was frequently accused of being a computer game fanatic by a father who wanted me to be a doctor! I asked myself, 'Why do parents want to clone their kids, why not allow them some individuality?'

Yes, at the time both my parents were frantic for me to fit in with their ideas. They were aware that I was possibly quite immature for my penultimate year before my 18th birthday and the invisible idea of reaching something called, Coming of Age.

But, then I suddenly thought, Liverpool and Anfield should be interesting and I quite liked the music scene coming out of somewhere called the Baltic Exchange; it had seemed to me to be vibrant, and a world away from the Beatle mania of the past. So, holding my breath, I announced my intention of putting Liverpool down as my first choice, and to make certain it was to be Liverpool, I put the Liverpool University as number one, John Moores University as second, and Hope University College for my third choice.

The real shock came when I suggested Liverpool; the parents didn't object! There was a sea change in the atmosphere. Dad in particular was the most impressed.

"Well, you should be safe enough there, if anything goes wrong you can drop by on my Uncle Gareth and Aunt Isobel."

"They must be one hundred and ninety, if they're a day!" I had moaned to all and sundry, until my cousin Rob whispered,

"No, you've got it all wrong Freddie, they're great, but you don't have to go anywhere near them. That's the whole point of going to Uni, get away from the family, stand on your own two feet, and find out about life, that's what my mother told me."

At last, advice I could follow. Robert Houghton the offspring of my Uncle Tim and Aunt Annie, and a direct descendant from the gallant and much be-medalled brave Philip and the even more amazing Annette Bedford, his wife.

But it was Annette's daughter-in-law and Rob's mother the fabulous Aunt Annie whose advice I would willingly choose to follow. If that is what his mother had told Rob, I knew it would be sound advice: was she not the most grounded member of the family, full of fun, loved dressing up when we messed around at charades. She was Boss! Sorry, is that a bit out of date, but you know what I mean? Later, I realized that as she was only a Houghton courtesy of the man she had married, Annie had joined the clan with a different set of values. Fortunately for her, she had married my Uncle Tim who was so laid back he sometimes seemed asleep and I always felt a kinship with him by that very fact.

Encouraged by my cousins, I did as the careers master suggested and found myself, after moderate 'A Level' results at that amazing Northern Redbrick, in the centre of Liverpool, studying the history of the 20th century, and slumming it with seven other students: three guys and four girls, in a large house halfway down the Smithtown Road. It was convenient: with an easy bus route into the centre of town, to lectures, to plenty of sports facilities and I know what you're going to say, I stopped off at the pub that is supposedly located on every street corner in Liverpool! But, I didn't actually drink in every pub that I came across, besides which, there was that magnificent Students' Union where the price was right and the girls were even better, and I was to quickly discover the café culture of Liverpool was certainly better than Basildon.

I cannot pretend that I worked hard, but I managed to survive the work that was asked of me. Somehow or other I found the ability to last out the first year and in spite of all my character faults, most notably bad timekeeping, and an inability to get out of bed in the morning, I returned for the second year without having to resort to a course change, history was still my option, even though my father was wondering what on earth I would do with it for a career, until I placated him with the lie that it had been mostly the study of military history, he grunted with a half-smile on his face saying, 'Good, good, yes, well done!'

That he swallowed that lie, is neither here nor there because I had willingly returned to university not because I lived to study, but because I loved the crowd I'm living with, the girls in particular were very good at frequently ignoring my lazy attitude towards washing up. It was my idea of domestic bliss, being surrounded by pretty girls, living in the only student digs with a dishwasher, a real dishwasher!

Looking back on that time, I realize that it was very much a game: playing at being grown up, believing that personal freedom equated with the idea that self-indulgence was the sole mark of a man's maturity.

Chapter 2

The Gauntlet is thrown down by the Professor.

Now, after all I've said about myself, you cannot dispute that I was basically a fairly lazy sort of chap, so that when the subject matter of the Second World War came up and my tutor Mr Edward Greenfield, dished out the challenge of writing an essay or thesis, call it what you will, based upon the memories of a living person and their experiences of World War Two, I groaned with frustration and kicked off the theory that I believed that everything that ever needed to be said about the Second World War had already been said, or written about in books and films.

Opening my hands as if in a gesture of despair, I heard myself sounding a tad like my Dad, as I asked, 'Why?' Then I distinctly remember I developed even more of the tone and mannerisms of my father as I continued with a new found verbosity.

"And furthermore, Sir, how does anyone sift through the garbage that old people come out with, as they try desperately to relive their past

lives. Is it possible for anyone to tell the difference between their fantasies and the modest realities that are the residual knowledge held within the fossilised brains of old people?"

Trying to sound intelligent, I knew I was play-acting and that at that moment, I was enjoying mimicking my Father with his extensive vocabulary, which I was borrowing in an attempt to deliver my objections with all the eloquence of a neuro-surgeon and I played the Thames Estuary southern accent with a virtuoso superiority, such a mean trick, but I enjoyed it!

Arrogant young fool! I could hear him thinking it and you saying it! He certainly looked as if he believed I was the one missing some marbles.

Meanwhile, I stared at him trying to look interested in what he was suggesting when truthfully I was still thinking, 'boring!'

But, then I half woke up when he continued.

'I want you to see it through the eyes of just one living person, initially no books, no surfing the

net, just focus on one person. Get on your bike and discover someone who lived through it. Find out what happened to them during and then after the war. Call it repercussions, call it consequences, call it after-effects, call it what you will, but relate the Second World War to the present day, though the insights and memories of just one person. What affected his life because of the war? Question him on the impact those early experiences had upon his subsequent life, and only then you may cross reference it to authenticated, known details.'

He pontificated yet more upon his theory about the elderly giving us their remembered emotions, which in his opinion would give historical facts a greater meaning, for us. He said that he felt I only saw history as a one dimensional disease instead of a vibrant collection of interrelated details, which could give the picture depth, colour and meaning and afforded a growth in our personal judgement; as we continued through our future life adventures. I tried not to appear frazzled by that bout of verbal diarrhoea. I thought he's just trying to say that we must learn by another's mistakes!

A week later, at my next seminar and having thought about his suggestions, I challenged him, admitting defeat and waiting for the bomb to drop, but, it didn't happen. Instead, he said quite gently, as if talking with a friend. "Listen young man, history has come to that point where those of us still living have one last chance to probe the memories of those who lived through that conflict."

By now he was strolling about his office in full flight of fancy, I was slouching there, hands in pockets, trying to worm my way out of the project, when he said,
"Do you realise young man," he continued in that unfamiliar and somewhat dramatic manner, even as I looked up into his face. I was staring at him as if in disbelief, until he suddenly said,

"... And the other day a man died who was known, recognised, as the last living Tommy from the First World War. Now there is no one left alive that actually experienced life in the trenches: it's gone and all that is left are letters, notes and the official reports of that time. What a wuste!" Suddenly he seemed more human as if he did still live in the real world, adding,

"How I would have loved to have sat with that man, found out what he really remembered of his experiences. He would have given sound to the newsreels for there was no sound, just the black and white moving image, like the silent movies that they were and people could only experience the soldiers' emotions because of the music that is superimposed upon the image. Yes, that is all that is left of the War to end all Wars, silence in black and white."

He sat down opposite me, crossing his legs and leaning back in his chair with his hands clasped across his belly, he looked totally content with life, as if like my father, he had got to that point in the conversation where he was speaking about his favourite topic.

"We need to look beyond the political thought that motivated the conflict and hear the real deep down feelings of the fighters, if we want to experience it as an emotional event happening to real men. It seems that all we have left, yes, all we have left is something as ridiculous as 'Black Adder' to remind us that those Tommie's were flesh and blood with real feelings, as they climbed

over the top, and not a silent one dimensional celluloid automaton. Did you never see 'Black Adder?' That final episode had me in tears, probably the most realistic portrayal of that war, we will ever see."

He paused looking at me as if trying to turn a key inside my head and I could think of nothing to say, then it struck me,

"Well Prof, how about 'Oh, What a Lovely War?' That goes a bit far, some people think it's a comedy, but I felt some serious emotions as I watched it."

"Did you really? What did you feel?" There was warmth in his tone: I felt secure in my reply.

"That it was senselessly chaotic: it was as if schoolboys were organising a football match, a rugby match, or a game of cricket and the referee wasn't there. If the master wasn't watching it would be chaos in such circumstances, if you can see what I'm trying to say, Sir."

"Good, good, good... that's a start. You realise that war is about people, just as much as it is about politics."

Then he reminded me that 2015 was 70 years on from the end of the Second World War and with luck I should be able to find someone over 70 who had a memory of living through that war.

As I've already told you: I was still a laid-back lazy minded excuse of a human being, so, thinking he would excuse me from the whole exercise, if I challenged him with a silly idea, I flippantly chimed up with, 'My Great Aunt lived through it,' was that a stupid thing to say? 'She didn't fight, like, but my dad says she is always nattering on about the war.'

It the silence that followed I thought I had won!

But, knock me down with a feather; all of a sudden he looked back at me, his eyes shining as if he had just been handed a Lottery win, as he said,

'You've fallen on your feet; you are a lucky guy, Frederick Woods! So get out there and interview her. Has she still got all her marbles?'

Now there he had me, I'd seldom met the old girl, but if she was like those of the family I had met, well my heart was in my boots! My family at that time was spread all over the country. I had Great Aunts and Uncles as far north as Durham, as far south as Chichester, and if you wanted East and West, well there was one in Norwich, and yes, there was Great Aunt Isobel and her youngest brother, my Great Uncle Gareth, living in Liverpool. I believe I was 12 the last time I saw them, I said nothing to them, I ran away having seen them ruffle Robert's hair and chuck Angela's already pink cheeks. They had looked ancient then; heaven only knows what they would look like now.

I sat there looking at my tutor and wondering how on earth I would approach the question of inviting myself into their home. In all the time I had lived in Liverpool, I had not once gone near them. I didn't even know if they knew that I was in the city. Surprisingly enough my Great-Aunt Isobel and Great-Uncle Gareth lived *not a mile away from my university digs. It was at that point that I suddenly felt overcome with embarrassment, I was in my second year at Uni and, as I just said, I have not once visited them. I believe I felt myself blush as I told my tutor of my rather negligent behaviour. He had laughed and said, "You're no different to the rest of your generation, Freddie. Get out there and see what they have to say."*

I searched for my address book, my mother had given it to me the day I began Uni, and it was loaded with contact details of all the relatives with notes alongside as to their potential usefulness. Could I find it? It took a while, before I was ready to admit that it was probably lost to the garbage bin and that in the end I would have to ring mother to get details of Uncle Gareth's phone number. Naturally she chided me for not having visited the old couple before, but as always I was full of excuses and reassured her that this time I really intended to ring Uncle Gareth.

Looking back I can't believe that I felt so nervous about the whole thing, but eventually I rang Uncle Gareth to test out the possibility of imposing myself upon them, while I did my research. With luck, I could fit it into the Michaelmas reading week, and let's be honest, I knew that my funds were running low and a week of free food would be very satisfying, Uncle Gareth was reputably a brilliant cook.

Mother was annoyed that I wasn't coming home for the week, and to my everlasting surprise, father laughed and said,

"You won't last a day Freddie, she's an ogre!'

But I did, and it was a week I will never forget. My Aunt Isobel was in her late 70s and believed herself to be a writer. She's my father's Aunt and he says she writes silly stories, and even more pointless plays, and nobody's ever heard of her: apparently her heyday was thirty or forty years ago. She still lives like a hermit in the back bedroom of Uncle Gareth's house, her younger brother who cares for her with a patience that my parents find stoically admirable and which I believe I could never produce within myself, should I be called upon to care for an elderly relative.

Thank goodness I'm an only child! I had eventually sussed out that I would marry and park my parents in a Grannie flat under the protection of my future wife, should I be unfortunate enough to find myself with parents with senility oozing out of their pores. And yes, I was fully confident that I would find the right woman to care for them. I can hear you; the list is growing, lazy, arrogant, and selfish!

But I will remember that week with total affection; both of them were complete individual characters who batted off each other with great humour. It was a week I look back on and remind myself that we had laughed every day, at breakfast time when Uncle Gareth teased me about my bad timing, right through till after supper when they had lights out at 10 o'clock. Yes, I lived within the frame work of their routine for a whole week, and I am prepared to admit that it was the first time in my life when I had such discipline imposed upon me, without my complaining about it.

Today I ppreciate that those two dear people taught me a great deal about life: taught me that if I was to succeed in life I had to impose some discipline upon myself, and yet it was all done with a gentle sweetness that I have seldom encountered in any other person since. Both of them lived by caring for each other and for a whole week I was in between them and thoroughly enjoying myself. I felt cocooned, safe, until I gradually relaxed to the point, when I knew that at long last I was going to write about real history, because I was beginning to understand what history means to genuine people. There was nothing Hollywood, Bollywood or Elstree in their presentation of the truth of themselves.

Isobel's memory was a sharp as a Samurai Katana bladed sword. You did not argue with her, but occasionally you had to duck and dive while she elaborated upon her very definite opinions on the subject of the war and its aftermath. There, it was, quite naturally and without fuss that Isobel Houghton gave me the word that inspired me to continue, it was when she unwittingly used the word that I was to pick up and use to designate the substance of what was to become my book.

Aftermath: the Second World War through the Eyes of a Child.

Chapter 3

Isobel remembers, Gareth feeds Freddie, and Freddie begins to understand.

If writers tell you that it is very difficult to find the title to a piece of work, let me assure you it is true. I don't know why, but even before I had arrived at their home, all I could think about was, 'What should I call this piece of work?' The dreaded title, always the torture in an author's mind! It equates to the editor's choice of front page headlines. Get it wrong and the paper doesn't sell: get it right and it sells like hotcakes.

I didn't want it to be one of the words that my tutor had put in front of me; what were they now? Yes, Repercussions, I didn't like that, it was too long and as for Consequences, that was a game we often played with silly sexual overtones, as we sat about the lounge of our student digs, drinking cheap cider until three in the morning.

It had been with some foresight that I was able to register the possibility that I would need something to help me deal with the whole situation. Consequently, I had borrowed a tape recording machine from the University: I loaded myself up with notepaper, ballpoint pens, and mobile phone. In the end, the latter was not used. Never for one second did I feel the need to escape from their company which was anything but claustrophobic, because I found it astonishingly stimulating and I felt an enthusiasm that was both surprising and fulfilling and now I believe it was during that week when I finally grew up, laughing and happy and learning that a bit of irreverence mingled with the ability to know when to be serious, were both healthy qualities for survival.

I arrived at their large terraced home, on the edge of Sefton Park and found myself surprised that the immediate impression was of a traditional late Victorian home full of artworks, of old heavy English oak furniture, with Turkish style rugs covering a pale coloured fitted carpet, and endless photographs of men and women in different uniforms. Make no mistake, the walls and furniture exhibited many different photographs of military personnel, I recognised one photo as my Great – Great - Uncle Harry who died in the First World War, I recognised others, there was Walter and Stanley, Great-Uncle's killed in the Second World War. There was my Great-Grandfather Philip in his army uniform, in a silver frame standing on a mahogany sideboard beside the photo of my Grandmother Alison who had worked as an Army nurse during the battle for the Falklands. There were others I did not immediately recognise, but I knew that I would be able to ask and find out their stories. In my Aunt Isobel's room there was one particularly beautiful photograph of her brother Gareth in his RAF uniform, positioned on the wall above her desk and beside that photograph there was another of two men in RAF uniform, I recognised one as Matt's Grandfather Charles and the other as his father Peter. Charles had died when I was young and I have no memory of him, but Peter I still see at family reunions. He is still in service in Germany.

When you live in untidy student digs, I suppose it was natural to be stunned by the very neatness and artistry that the old couple had created as their home. It was probably the most comfortable place I'd ever been into, not even my parent's house, a very modern post war new build with everything reduced to create the minimum amount of trouble when trying to clean it, could I describe as giving such a feeling of luxury and comfort as that which seemed to exude from every corner of Isobel and Gareth's house. Everything was like a tribute to the Edwardian era, although Gareth explained later that most of their furniture was an amalgamation of hand-me-downs from several generations born in the previous two centuries,

"Fortunately, we both like the familiarity of things which to us have a story, we may not know their names but we do know their homes look something similar to this. We believe most of it is from our Great Grandmother's time, dealers tell us it is probably 1820. Worth keeping don't you think?"

There was such a twinkle in his eyes as he said that and I smiled back asking, "Do you know her name?" "Of course I do, would you like to see the family tree?"

Something flipped over inside of me as he had asked me. I nodded my head, but I think it was the expression on my face that really gave him confirmation of my eagerness to see the document. Well, I assumed it was a document, how naive can you be, it turned out to be an almost poster size framed parchment with no resemblance to any A4 sheet of computerized *printout, that I had imagined was to be produced by him.*

'Wow!'

'Yes, it's large. This is known as an AO poster size, difficult to get hold of these days unless you go to specialist print shop. I made this up with the help of the family, but it might be useful this week, so I think I'll leave it down here and we can refer to it as we talk about the family. Will that be all right with you?'

In that moment of courtesy, I felt something I had never experience before: I had the choice to agree or not, and either way would be fine with this friendly older man.

I had arranged to arrive there by midday on the Friday, and once I had settled my bag in the bedroom to which I had been shown, I quickly joined them for Friday lunch. I was surprised to find that I would have called that a full dinner: their day is upside down to my usual pattern of eating. I was to discover the pleasure of breakfast, dinner, afternoon tea and a snack just before bedtime. Even the food was completely traditional and perfect. Uncle Gareth, a campaigner for the health giving properties of butter, refused to allow margarine in the house; he despised all processed food and believed in what he called proper cooking.

That first afternoon I sat at the table and watched him serve us with beautifully poached haddock topped by an egg and accompanied by new potatoes, all cut and shaped to the same size, and when I queried them, he explained that they were Châteaux potatoes while the peas were called petite pois and the carrots were, a la Julienne. There was no sauce, they were all floating in a delightfully mint flavoured butter. Portions were not large and because he was worried that I might be hungry, I had the addition of several slices of freshly buttered home-made bread. As we ate, the conversation was not forced, but it was friendly and jolly and I realised that I was not going to be bored. They both laughed a lot, they each asked me different questions about what it was like to go to university in the 21st-century and by the time we had finished a modest Queen of Puddings, and downed at least two cups of tea, I knew that if I just relaxed, went with the flow, as we say, I would survive. Why did I keep using that word, survive? Was it built into my juvenile mind that old people were a challenge? Isobel and Gareth certainly did not resemble the image that I had in my mind from my parent's collection of photographs.

Isobel was short, yes, tiny but stout, with a rather dated choice of clothing. In fact there was nothing modern about her beyond the fact that she liked red lipstick. Her untidy grey hair never bothered her, but I soon learnt that it irritated her brother who kept reminding her to brush her hair. It was as if every day she got up and it was the one thing she didn't think about, brushing her hair. But she was sweet and I soon fell in love with her.

When examining the Family Tree it clearly stated, Isobel was born in January 1940, during one of the coldest winters so far recorded for the twentieth century.

"But, you see Freddie; I don't count that as the beginning. How could it be? I have no memory of being born; to me, my life began with my first memories. Freddie, none of us remember being born, and certainly for the first couple of years my

life I wasn't truly conscious of what was going on in the world. Nothing odd in that, it's called being a baby, then a toddler, and somewhere in the middle of being a toddler you discover that you notice things, but you can never be certain that your memory of them is yours or what your parents have told you had happened in your infancy. My earliest recollection of my own, from my childhood, was when I was two and a half. I more than vaguely remember seeing your Great-Uncle Eddie, who at only 13 months, and already an efficient walker, who had wandered down to the gate, just as three geese came walking past. I remember mother shouting at him 'Eddie stop that comeback here,' but no he stuck his hand through the gate and got his finger bitten by one of the geese walking past. Years later I discovered the truth and that, I had not imagined it. We had in fact been living in a cottage near Ingatestone in Essex. We had been evacuated there to avoid the Battle of Britain, or so I was told, but it seems odd, we had only travelled less than 20 miles from our home in Vange."

Isobel paused and took a sip of her tea; I think she almost forgot that I was there. It occurred to me that perhaps I should ask a question, but no I sat in silence and waited. After a while she seemed to remember that I was there so I just let the tape run and she soon talked on as if in a dream, her world as Gareth called it. It was strange, as if the old dear had been rehearsing her story until it was word perfect.

"There have been images remembered of a man in uniform and I remember a car journey. Years later, Mother had said, that I was remembering true incidents and that much of it was after the Battle of Britain, during the period before we returned home. I suppose today, we might think such a move as unwise. Yes, we may say, we had gone back home to our Basildon home, only a bus ride away from factories at Dagenham, and the Thames Docks, before we should have done; it had been too soon to guarantee our complete safety. But, because the Battle of Britain had seemed so dramatic, and the winter of 1940 had been so very cold mother found the apparent calmness that followed, less frightening. Mind you, I still think the real reason was she was lonely and missing her sister. Momentarily, Hitler seemed less interested in the nightly bombing of our part of England: was it that somehow or other we had become better at

getting the sirens up and running. I don't really know, but I do believe it was that we all somehow got used to it.

Does it seem strange to you that a journey of little more than 20 miles north had taken mother beyond the fear of the Luftwaffe and even though it was still in the Essex countryside it had at first been a comfort to her? But, eventually she had to get back to her family, evacuation was all very well but my mother always spoke of how lonely it was in a tiny two-bedroom cottage with no hot water, no heating and actually no electricity. I think the dark scared her as much as anything. It was my belief that she came home because she couldn't face another winter in there and she missed her sister. We've still got the stone hot water bottles, I've put one in your bed, and you must tell Gareth if it needs topping up."

If she stopped to take breath I hardly noticed by now I was almost hypnotised by the quality of her speaking voice. It isn't often that you come across someone who truly speaks with the love of the language they are using, and an appreciation of the effect of the voice on the listener. Isobel had a voice that echoed with culture and class; and yet she would have been the first to acknowledge her-self as working class.

"But do you know, Freddie, the realization of what was going on in the real world first hit me squarely between the eyes in December 1943, yes it was one month short my fourth birthday. Put bluntly, Hitler's onslaught intensified as new weapons, gave him hope of fulfilling his dream of conquering Britain; and in the process not only threatening to destroy the Houghton home, but frightening all of us with the possibility of death, as flying bomb after flying bomb rained down upon our little country, mostly in the daytime, but sometimes in the dead of night.

I always say that we live on a very small island. My childish memory is of asking Mother why Hitler wanted England when he already had Germany, which according to Charlie's atlas showed an enormous area coloured green and twice the size of the little patch of red which included England.

'We are British' said Mother, 'and we will never give in, Mr Churchill has said so.'

Naturally we believed that both Mother and Mr Churchill knew what they were talking about."

She smiled at me, and suddenly laughed as she said,

"If only Google Earth had been available to Hitler, he would have known that he was targeting a part of the world that was no great threat to him. Truly he was trying to reach not only the docks, but also factories such as Ford's Motors or Plessey's engineering works, all producing important hardware for the army. Then there were the politically important sites such as the Houses of Parliament or Buckingham Palace, but even at three years and eleven months, I was old enough to understand much of what was happening and could ask the question, "Why is our house important to Hitler?"

Suddenly Isobel was rummaging through a box of grainy black and white snapshots. They were all well-worn; I suppose a sign of how important they were to her. The one she selected I recognised immediately, still the home of my Great Uncle Charles, but back then, that of my

Great, Great Grandparents, I knew that they had all lived there at various times.

"Do you remember the photograph of the old family home? Yes, the Victorian terraced one. Mother once explained to Charlie and I that we were living under a cloud called Hitler's flight path. And Hitler and his flight path became the objects of our hatred. Yes, I truly hated Hitler and I wasn't yet four! I feared for our lives and I feared for a house, which I loved, and look around here now. Freddie that bookcase survived: so did we, but it wasn't easy. Do you want to know more?"

"Auntie, it's just lovely please go on. Please tell me everything, it doesn't matter, you can muddle it all up, I'll sort it out later. What was it that happened that December 1943?"

"Our home was large and we all lived in various parts of it. We all slept downstairs in one very large room to the right of the front door, and my Mother's sister had rooms upstairs; I remember they had a full sized billiard table in one of their rooms.

I loved drawing pictures of my home. Always from that time until now, that first memory of my home was to be my abiding image *of what a proper house should be. Victorian! Today, as you can see, I still live in a Victorian House, not as large as that first one, but sufficiently solid and tranquil to remind me of home. That it is over two hundred miles away from the town where I was born does not bother me, somehow the familiarity resides in the bricks, in the room sizes and even in the pattern created by the floor tiles in the porch. Here, look at this, as it was in the 1930's, it was taken by your Great-Grandfather using his old box brownie, you know what that is," she said with a smile.*

Isobel was ready to talk again, and as I handed back that photograph or should I call it the snapshot, she began,

"Even in wartime my mother polished that letter box, and I remember my three year old face smiling back at myself. That day I waited for Mummy to insert the key and open the door to reveal the wonders of that colourful Victorian encaustic tiled floor; perfectly scrubbed clean and stretching to what seemed a mile away, towards the green painted backdoor, leading onto our adventure garden."

I let her talk on. There were words I had never heard before, but time enough to ask later. I kept a careful watch on my tape recorder. I did not want to miss anything, I had a feeling that everything about to be said was going to have some significance for my essay.

"That day, the December sun was shining down from the landing window, highlighting through the panels of its deep cerulean blue coloured glass which surrounded the central pane, the reds, yellows, blues and black of that wonderful floor. On that day, it was perfection, with the smell of lavender furniture polish, of the smoky coal fire in the back sitting room. And there was cabbage, I hate the smell of cabbage, it's so intense, cabbage always seemed to permeate the house; but on that day it was all mixed together into a heavy, almost evil sickly sweetness, from the slow baking of a Christmas cake, now over-cooked and very near to burning, in our kitchen. Today, I still remember that Christmas cake, the recipe was one Mummy had adapted from the Be-ro recipe book. There were a few pieces of dried fruit, a great deal of grated suet and lots of grated carrots and other vegetables, which she described as her own inventive contribution to the

War on Want. Mummy said, "We'll not spoil Christmas just to please Mr Hitler, oh no, we support Mr Churchill in this house, make do and mend includes our Christmas cake!"

"Oh, Freddie, there have been many times when the memory of Mummy almost pontificating her thoughts and beliefs over the noise of our play, comes flooding back into my mind. Today I believe it was her way of softening the loneliness of her life: father was away fighting and she missed him. She seldom sounded as if she was speaking to us; I do now believe she was speaking in her heart to Philip, her husband and our father, your Great Grandfather."

She paused again, her eyes looking out into the distance, but they didn't seem to be focused on anything in particular, and yet I knew that she was remembering very clearly. Suddenly she said,

"Well, back to the cake! It was coloured with gravy browning to make it look rich and fruity, and honestly, after that long slow cook, it came out of the oven as heavy as a brick. I remember my Nana said, 'Too much suet, dear.'

But it was Christmas Eve 1943 and we were still alive, and determined to celebrate, just in case Daddy got home for Christmas. The concept of disappointment at the burnt cake never reached our young minds, we often ate burnt toast, and you just scraped the black off and ate it because you could not afford to throw away even the burnt crusts off your toast. Do you know, Freddie that we cleaned our teeth every day with a mixture of salt and soot taken from inside the chimney flue. I hear you Freddie, laugh away: but who had access to toothpaste? Only the very rich! What you never had, you didn't miss! In fact my Christmas wish, as I stirred the cake, was for Daddy to be home for Christmas. Charlie had been first to make his Christmas cake wish, he managed to reach into the mixing bowl while still standing on his own two feet, but then he was very nearly six and went to school. I on the other hand, had to kneel up on a chair and little Eddie; well he had to be held up by Mummy. I do believe we all had the same Christmas wish; it would be a fair assumption because Mummy more or less said the words with each of us. 'I wish Daddy would be home for Christmas.'

Then in the living room, we had set up a crib in celebration of the birth of the Saviour. Placed on the oak sideboard, we had made a little crib out of a cardboard box covered in screwed up brown paper. It didn't matter if postage marks or the occasional stamp was showing, we never noticed as the wonder of the Christmas story grew in front of our eyes. Mummy produced all the Nativity figures, except the Infant Jesus.

"Where is the baby?" we had demanded.

"Jesus will be born during the night," she had solemnly declared.

But we didn't mind, there was enough to look at as we gazed at the coloured plaster figures no more than two inches tall and as ancient as could be; the missing nose on a king was no matter, any more than the nob broken off the top of the jar of frankincense. When you are coming up to your fourth birthday, only a month away, you had the imagination to fill in the missing details."

I smiled at her and reminded her that my Dad still has that crib, so I knew exactly what she was talking about, but she didn't seem to notice me, now it was almost as if she was writing her memoirs, even as she spoke.

"That night before bed, the three of us gathered around Mummy, as she led us through the words and music of 'Away in a Manger' and I remember that as we sat in that darkened room, lit by our Christmas candle, placed beside the crib, and awaiting the Baby Jesus; Mummy explained that the candle was to show Jesus the way and also to guide all travellers out on that cold and windy night, who were trying to get home to spend Christmas with their loved ones. As that included Daddy we were excited at the prospect. Forever after, whenever spending Christmas in my own home, I would light a candle to show the traveller the way home. Don't ask me why I do so, but it is like a prayer for those struggling against the odds to get back to those who love them and would miss them on that sacred night. Then Mummy hustled us across the hall to the communal ground floor bedroom, where we all slept cheek by jowl and she helped us hang a sock on the end of each of our beds, awaiting Father Christmas and his bounty. It was wartime and we were full of questions.

"No, dear, Hitler cannot kill Father Christmas, he'll be flying over with your presents, when you are asleep, now go to sleep."

"But, if one of the bombs hit the reindeer," we argued and fretted for hours. Charlie was certain that Rudolf would be able to dodge any bomb crossing his route. Eddie still worried, he was not yet three and promised to stay awake all night to make sure Father Christmas ate the biscuit and drank his glass of milk. Mummy tucked us up; checking that our bundles, our shoes and our slippers were all placed ready for a speedy exit should the siren sound off.

I don't remember much of that actual Christmas Day beyond the disappointment of an absent father, but I do remember walking miles to the Church in the High Street, wearing my gift from Father Christmas. My stocking had been filled with an apple, two toffees, a pencil and two ribbons for my hair. But, wrapped in a brown paper parcel was a dress. It looked familiar, it was a hand me down once worn by Cousin Angela. I loved it and constantly whirled round and round to see the hem swing out. I imagined I was a dancer, I was so happy with my present. The daily ritual of dressing my hair with ribbons was always a moment when we could all marvel at our Mummy's skill as a hairdresser. For Christmas, that year, I distinctly remember the white ribbons

Mummy had somehow acquired for me. She brushed my hair and then there was usually a centre parting, then from each side a plait would be made and crossed over the back of my head to lead into more plaits which, when finished were looped up and the whole secured by the large ribbon bows. By the time I was four my hair was reaching my waist, but then I was fairly short, so I suppose it wasn't as massively long as my four year old self remembers. Somewhere along the line and taking a relative view of myself, my hair has always been important to me. I am pleased I still have a reasonable amount on my head, now I'm 75. Do I wish it was still as blackish brown as it had been all those years ago? Possibly, but I'm told it is silver now. I think it is just grey."

My Aunt seemed unstoppable, but I held my hand up for a moment to signify that I needed to change the tape. She smiled at me and when I gave her the signal to begin again she was off as if the interruption had meant nothing.

"You have so many things to use these days all with buttons and dials I can't keep up with it. There wasn't any television in those days and the radio was never continuously blaring out music, the way so many households cover the silence of *their meaningless lives, today. At that time, the news was listened to by Mummy, but I took no notice. It was just a voice, a man with gruff speech who always seemed to make Mummy frown and sigh and tut with an annoyance which did not suit her, for she was a beautiful woman. Her smile was legendary and she and her sisters were always spoken of as 'The Vange Sisters' as if they were as famous as the Andrews sisters, they were American singers whose 78rmp records Mummy sometimes played on a Sunday after teatime. It was the musical treat we looked forward to, because there were always familiar songs, songs I still love."*

Suddenly she was very quiet, very still, in some ways looking sad, until something prompted her to start humming a tune. I did not at first recognise it but then she changed to another and I knew it was one of Vera Lynn's, I think, yes, I'm almost certain it was something I once heard called 'On a Wing and a Prayer.' Suddenly, she seemed to sag, as if exhausted, and I felt obliged to ask if she wanted to stop.

"Auntie, do you want to rest now, we've got all week, it's alright you don't have to talk it all out in one afternoon."

She was laughing at me, I could tell. Suddenly she leaned across and took hold of my hand before pulling me until I was kneeling in front of her.

'Sing to me,' she said with a mischievous grin. I couldn't help myself, I was grinning back at her, 'I don't think you would like what I like,' I said, knowing I sounded somewhat feeble.

'What's your favourite song?' She asked me and I replied, 'Well, not one you would know.'

'Try me' she said, still with laughter in her voice, 'Do you listen to the radio?'

'No Auntie, I use Spotify,'

'Good grief what's that?'

'Do you know what an App is?'

'Well, Gareth keeps trying to show me his amazing phone which is apparently full of Apps. So I suppose, am I right in saying your Spotify is a web program?'

'Yes and my favourite singer at the moment is a man called Sam Smith.'

'And your favourite song?'

'Stay with me! Have you heard it?'

She smiled, and gave me an affectionate pat on the top of my head, before saying,

'No, darling boy these days I don't listen to pop music, I can't understand the words, I like to be able to sing along, you can't do that with modern music.'

All of a sudden Isobel sagged as if drained of life; she leant back in her chair and closed her eyes.

'Auntie would you like to stop and have a rest, it's alright.'

Famous last words, suddenly she sat up smiled, and carried on again, eyes looking out, past the net curtains at the window, out into some far beyond place where she felt very real, very much alive. I switched the tape on again.

"In our home, Kathleen Ferrier was as popular as Vera Lynn and my brothers and I sang along to the likes of 'Red Sails in the Sunset' and 'We'll meet again, don't know where, don't know when,' with all the gusto of our childhood innocence, not fully realizing the meaning of the words, just knowing that our Mummy seemed

different as she sang along with the music and her eyes constantly straying to the photographs displayed on the mantelpiece."

Isobel's head turned and she looked straight into my eyes, I could see the tears forming and I felt her fear. I felt a shiver permeate up my spine as I realised how deep her emotions were affecting her at that moment.

I stayed silent, immobile, and then she took off again with such firmness in her voice that I knew it was important. I sat back again and I switched the tape on.

"More and more there were the sirens blaring out warnings of approaching destruction. My sister, Alison, your Grandmother, was born early in 1944 and even before her birth everything had begun to change. Hitler had apparently invented a new bomb. The adults around me spoke of him as the greatest evil in the world, the destroyer, the killer and numerous other words which my young mind accepted as evidence that Hitler was the worst bad man alive. Not even Stalin was mentioned, I would have remembered. Then Mr Churchill was the other name Mummy and her sisters often mentioned. Thus it was, that

Hitler was our bogey man, and Churchill, sorry, Mister Churchill was the man we obeyed, because he was looking after our Daddy."

It amused me how all of a sudden her voice seemed to change its tone and she appeared to be younger than ever, almost childlike as she said 'Mister' when speaking of Churchill. Strangely enough the light was fading as evening drew in, and I made no effort to switch on a light. We sat in the gloom and somehow as she spoke it seemed even more real; I found that I had begun to feel a shudder going up my spine as her voice conveyed her childlike fears of what was happening at that time. It felt as if it was less of the memory and more of a reality. In that moment I understood why I had been asked to write this essay, I felt I was living with her, way, ... way back, ... in the war. I felt her fears.

"We prayed for Daddy and Mister Churchill. Sometimes our ritual prayers would seem naïve by today's standards. 'God bless Mummy and Daddy and all kind friends and relations. Help Mr Churchill to look after Daddy. And may our guardian angels watch over us this night.' The siren would begin its whining noise as it grew and grew until it seemed to take over all the space in the house.

Her hands lifted and waved as if pointing to the four corners of the ceiling. But I knew she was seeing her childhood home. It was real to her, and I felt I was there with her. She carried on her voice changing with each phrase; and I knew which one was speaking, by her voice. Her mother began the conversation:

"You have to go to the shelter,

'Don't want to.' That would be Charlie.

'Who says so?' That would be me.

'Mister Churchill says so.' That was our Mummy.

'Why?' chorus of Charlie, Eddie and me.

'To save us from that nasty man called Mr Hitler!'

'It was all to become a logical reason to our young brains. Daytime was easy; we just ran out down the garden and sat in the shelter playing Cat's Cradle or snap. But in the dark at night, it was all so different. Bedtime meant a certain ritual that mother had ingrained into our young *minds: we had to know where everything was so that we could easily leave the house and reach the shelter, in the dark of the night without torches or candles. It began with the normal bedtime things such as how we went about undressing. First, we had to make a pile of our garments for a speedy and I mean speedy reaction, I mean an instantaneous reaction to the siren. We began by spreading our coat or jumper or cardigan at the end of the bed and on top of it each garment until the whole could be rolled up into a neat bundle to be placed against the end of the bed, and our dressing gown or coat was placed on top. I had to leave my liberty bodice on, day and night all winter, just as my brothers never removed their woollen vests. Pyjamas and nightdresses and cardigans worn as bed jackets in winter, all made us look like a gang of ragamuffins. Nothing new, all hand-me-downs from older cousins and friendly neighbours, but we were too young to care and when you are cold, the last thing any of us thought about was fashion. In winter, homemade scarves, balaclavas and mittens were de rigueur.*

Our shoes or slippers were placed precisely beneath the bed, to allow us to slide straight into them without any help. Looking back, I realise that… that you would say it was a Wallace and Gromit scenario, akin to the Wrong Trousers' episode. The siren would blare out its gathering message until it filled the whole street and woke us up. We were all silent, even at three years of age, and at three in the morning; fear caught at the back of your throat. Picking up our bundles we would hurry out of the bedroom and turn left down the darken passageway, until we reached the back door. Come rain or snow, we stood waiting for Mummy to arrive carrying Eddie who always seemed to be a little frightened by the siren; unlike six year old Charlie, who appeared to be sleepwalking throughout the whole exercise! I swear he never woke up. In fact, come morning he would wake in the Anderson shelter with a 'How did I get here?'

Each householder, usually with some help from friendly neighbours had erected those corrugated steel shelters in most of the back gardens of our road, and as we made our way to our shelter, we could hear various neighbours calling to each other, "You alright there, Mrs Brown?" "Jimmy, come on I can hear the doodlebugs." others were cursing either the weather or the war; it was their way of letting us know who was safely out of their house. And we all hated the rain and the cold. It always seemed to be raining.

Our shelter was like most of the others, half buried in the ground with a thin concrete floor, which sloped to the drainage hole: that was nothing more than a tube pushed down into the ground below to take any flooding, for when it rained the water flowed down the brick steps and under the door.

That's when slippers became a curse and my little feet would freeze. I remember the chilblains with horror and the blue legs that looked like the icicles which could be seen hanging down from wintery ledges below the frozen window ledges of our home.

Six people could rest in that shelter, there was a make shift two tier bunk bed that housed Charlie and Eddie on the top and myself and Nana when she was with us, on the lower level. But Mummy always sat upright on a rickety bench opposite us and always right next to the door. She would never shut it completely, her fear of the pitch blackness of the shelter, with the door closed, was obvious to us children. Sometimes I used to think she was simply watching to make certain our home was not bombed, as if she was trying to jinx the bombers, defying them to dare to fall on our road, our house.

I would fret and whisper, "Mummy is Rosie safe?" Rosie was another cousin, and they never left their home, they simply sheltered under Uncle Reg's billiard table. I can still hear her saying,

"Yes, dear, she'll be under the billiard table."

We all marvelled at their fearlessness; because they never come to join us in the garden. I worried because I knew the billiard table was strong, but just supposing its legs gave way and the whole thing squashed them. I knew what quashing things would do to them, had I not watched my brother collecting snails and worms to murder as substitutes for Mr Hitler.

Mummy tutted and sighed and sometimes you could hear her praying.

I would whisper, "Mummy, I can't sleep."

"Isobel, try and sleep, dear," she would say, as she leant over and wrapped a blanket around *me. But the blanket, as well as the cushions padding the hard wooden bunk, was always freezing cold, no matter what time of the day or night it was."*

Listening to all that, as it had poured out of her in a stream of consciousness, of memories so vivid that I felt I was there with her in the shelter, I now realise why it is so important to her to record what happened. It was obvious that those frightening memories made her feel alone inside her mind, even though she was in what novelists call 'the bosom of her family.'

"Didn't your Mum give you a nice warm cuddle?" I asked, remembering how many cuddles I had received as an only child. Something inside of me ached as I listened to this old lady speaking with obvious pain, as if the memory was worse than the actual experience of the bombing.

"Freddie, believe me, I have no cherished memories of being comforted by a cuddle, from my Mummy. Years later my brothers and sister and I would discuss this anomaly; a Mother who had so many children that the only way she could get on with her work was to ignore our longing for a cuddle. Yet she was never unloving; just

always avoiding the physical, where we were concerned. There were moments when the cold was so cold I thought I would freeze like the icicles hanging off the outside toilet cistern. Remembering it now, I often think to pray for what the world calls 'rough sleepers' for the memory of the cold and the discomfort of the shelter has stayed with me until this day, seventy years on."

Isobel laughed and gave me a gentle poke on my upper arm,

"Guess what, Mum kept a bucket in the shelter, for us to use as a potty, during the raids. Sometimes she must have wondered if it was worth the effort, most of us just wet ourselves as blast after blast shook the ground beneath the shelter. Charlie was the exception; he slept through everything and always woke to the excitement of his 'Street inspection!' Mummy, trying to bottle feed Alison, would listen patiently as he listed how many houses had broken windows and how many houses were reduced to rubble. Somehow I don't remember him mentioning bodies. That was left to adult neighbours who would pour in with the most important bits of the news. To me, Charlie seemed

fearless and one day he was to prove that he was indeed the man of the house."

By now it was dark, and Gareth came in, switching on the light. As he did so, both Isobel and I seemed almost shocked by the sudden intrusion of the light. It was time for tea.

A very different young man walked out of that sitting room that evening. I still felt as if I had sat in that air raid shelter. As if I had lived through that time. As if Hitler had tried to kill me. It was the weirdest concept I had ever experienced up to that point in my life.

Chapter 4

<u>The Bravery of Charlie</u>

The next day, I slipped out early to get more tapes for the recorder. There was no way I wanted to miss anything that Isobel had to say. I realized that it was better not to question her, just let her keep going until she dried; then let her snooze. Gareth said, "Let her nod off in little bouts, and she'll be Okay."

By ten o'clock we were back in the lounge with Isobel all scrubbed and pink cheeked. Garth laughed and said, "Ready for your boyfriend?" at which she smiled and turn sad eyes at me, saying, "He's nowhere as beautiful as my sweetheart!" Gareth laughed again and left the room. I said nothing as I set up the recorder and Isobel waited for my signal. My mind was amazed at how she had obviously thought through what she wanted to say and I just sat in silence, listening to her speaking as if from a book; she had planned it all. It was only when she stopped that I realized how significant the events of that day had been, not only to her, but to our family even to this day. It was beginning to dawn upon me some of the reasons behind my tutor's instructions for this piece of work. Again Great Aunt Isobel's voice went in and out of a childish treble set against a deeper more considered tone. She was reliving the events and I seemed forgotten as she proceeded with her story. Today I frequently re-listen to this tape and the next one, for I remember my own feelings, they had been incredibly powerful when I had first heard this part of her life story.

"Ready? Good! It was one of the most terrifying and poignant experiences of my childhood and still looms large in amongst my memories. The day was a warm spring day, bright and sunny. We were all happy after a reasonably quiet night, we had slept all night in our beds, so with Alison in the pram, and Charlie and Eddie dancing along in front of us, Mummy and I chatted as we headed off down our road towards 'Auntie' Mary's house near the Park. I cannot remember the number, but I could lead you to where the house was situated. It was opposite the gate nearest the road from Granary Lane. A large three bedroomed house with a front and back garden and on that day the adults were celebrating the new arrival, I believe it was a baby girl.

Uncle Jack and his Mummy were there, I remember them both; their image is impressed upon my memory as two smiling and friendly people. The two babies, Alison and the new-born, were passed around and much admired. We were fed a biscuit and a drink of what was called homemade lemonade, it was just a sickly pretence of beet sugar water coloured by carrot juice; before playing in the garden. I remember I went inside because I was tired after the long walk and then we had been playing tag in the garden.

Later, Mummy said I had saved her life because by going inside I got bored and started fidgeting, wanting to go home. But that wasn't entirely true. All I remember is that I had a strange feeling, an atmospheric feeling; the world seemed as if it wanted to spin and I begged Mummy to take us home.

"Home, Mummy, we have to go home,"

"Later dear, later,"

"No, now, Mummy, now!"

I persisted until Auntie Mary suggested that we all walked together to the shops, as she needed milk. Leaving 'Uncle Jack' and his Mummy to look after the baby, we set off with Julia and Paul, all of us skipping and playing another game of tag. I wasn't completely happy and at that time my hearing was excellent. I remember that I pulled on Mummy's dress and begged her to hurry.

The growling rumble that was the noise from the engine of a V1 rocket, grew and grew as it come from the east, heading for who knew where. So near it felt as if it was overhead and we all knew it was coming straight for us.

"Dear God, please, not us, keep it flying, please keep it flying." that was Mummy's prayer, said out loud, yes, out loud.

But, 'Auntie' looking upwards, realised as the engine cut out, that it was stopping over the Park. She screamed and began running back towards her home, but Charlie leapt at her and held her until the blast and the rumbling was over. How he did it, I would never know, but it helped her compose herself before walking back to the corner and together with Mummy, stand and watch the great cloud of dusty rubble spreading out above what had been Aunt's home. When at last it settled they moved in terror to the crater that had just moments before, been her home.

I was still holding on to the Silver Cross Pram with Alison sleeping through the noise, even as a fire engine could be heard coming towards us, I marvelled at Charlie organizing Julia, Paul and Eddie, herding them like sheep to a safe place, in a neighbouring front garden. I followed, awkward in my control of the pram, but successful on my third attempt to steer it through the gate and onto the path. We all stood there watching in fear, knowing there would be nothing to be happy about: we knew what had happened.

We were used to the noise of an exploding bomb, there had been so many in our short lifetime, but this one had seemed the loudest and was to prove one of the most devastating of bombs during my first four years of life.

The house was gone, the crater was a hole that stretched from what was the back garden and had obliterated their home as it continued across the road to the park gates; I couldn't see the pillars that had once held park gates. I remember I am now thinking maybe there never were any gates there; they were probably removed to make planes and bombs. There was little or no wind and the dust was already settling showing the truth. All was gone.

Mummy was clinging to Mary, now in hysterics and weeping in pain, as she sank to the ground. I remember her crying, "Jack, Jack!" and the baby's name, but I cannot remember the baby's name, only that as she was screaming it, people appeared. Some kind woman gathered us children up and took us into a house further away from the site.

For me the nightmare has never gone away, I remember what I saw in the rubble. I cannot tell you, the memory belongs to me alone. It hurts still. It added to my childlike hatred of that man called Hitler."

I remained still and silent as Isobel gave herself a few moments to remember that which was so horrible she could not speak of it. Then she straightened her back and I knew she was facing yet more painful memories with a stoicism that was truly admirable.

She began...

"That was the sadness of that month. And even as the spring was awakening and flowers waved in the breeze and seemed just as cheerful as they ever had to be, so that day I knew and understood the war was going to control my life even more than before. That night Mummy cried and I listened to her praying out loud that Mr Hitler would somehow or other be destroyed and we could live without fear.

Again, I must say that name 'Hitler' for he was the bogeyman that ruled our lives and took happiness away from my Mummy. He was the man who had that day killed a new born baby that I had only an hour before held in my arms. I knew what she should have looked like: I remember how little of her was left to bury.

I grew up that day, even though I was too young to know that the country was in a state of preparedness for the D Day landings and that our father was too far away to be of much comfort to Mummy. She and her sisters, all still living in and around South Essex, must have gone through hell during the period of those doodle bugs and the flying bombs. The sirens did not always give you proper warnings, it was nobody's fault; it was dependent upon how high or low the bombs were flying; for the radar could not track them if they were 'under' the operational height needed for the radar to work properly and the signal to be given. Within a matter of days we experienced another trauma caused by the suddenness of a flying bomb, which would seriously affect our little family. Not just for the day it happened, but for the rest of our Mummy's life.   I   must   tell you, Freddie of the day our home was blitzed."

Isobel sat almost frozen as the memories came piling back and fortunately for me Gareth entered and said it was time for lunch. We were all fairly quiet as we once again ate such beautifully cooked food. Somehow the other Isobel seemed to regain her strength, and after lunch I started the fifth tape and heaven help me, I was crying by the end of it. Isobel was calm and Gareth told me not to be anxious, he knew when she needed to rest, but realizing how far into her story she was, he opted to sit in on that afternoon session. I was glad; I was the one who needed his comforting.

Isobel looked at me in silence then nodded her head to indicate that she was ready. I switched the tape recorder on and sat watching her as she spoke, just glancing at the tape every now and them.

She began; "Again, there was no warning. It happened in a split second. Again no siren, again devastation was all around.

Charlie was in the pantry, a large walk in cupboard with shelves and only metal gauze for a window. It was our food store being always cold, winter and summer; we had no such luxury as a refrigerator or American Icebox.

The room itself was a large square room, big enough for a centrally placed table, under which Eddie sat. I do not remember what he was doing that day, but he always seemed to be playing with a ball. Usually a very worn and dirty tennis ball, which one of the Aunts had given him for Christmas.

Picture the room, entering from the hallway, the east facing window, heavily taped with a diagonal pattern of a masking tape, was on your right hand, with a large butler sink and wooden draining boards on either side, all centrally placed in front of the window. Various low level cupboards were both side and there were lidded buckets underneath the sink for *soaking soiled nappies. Carry on around the room and you passed the door to the walk-in pantry with its slate slab which acted as our refrigerator; next to the pantry door there was a large gas stove. It was blue in colour and had a top level grill, four gas rings and a large oven beneath. Mummy liked it, saying, "It's big enough to roast a turkey, if we only had enough coupons!" We would laugh and say we'd rather not eat a turkey, the picture of one in Charlie's farmyard story book made us all decide turkey was an ugly bird.*

"I don't eat ugly food," declared Charlie, and Eddie. I always agreed with Charlie, so I also appeared to upset Mummy by stating as adamantly as I could, that I would never eat an ugly animal. "One day you will realise how hard it is to feed growing children." I always remember her saying that if we played with our food instead of getting on with eating it.

The next wall around had chairs and the table coming out into the middle of the room. Turn the last corner, and there I was sitting on the floor, shelling peas into a metal colander and my back mercifully tucked against the side of the Welsh dresser, and my face turned away from the taped up window.

In the centre of the room, Mummy was sitting at the end of the table; with her back to the taped windows, bottle feeding Alison, whom I believe was by now about four months old when this event happened, because Mummy was already two months pregnant. I remember that! Daddy had had a flying visit to say goodbye before joining the Invasion we now call D.Day.

There was no siren as the window came in with such a force that the glass from between the tapes was hurled right across the whole width of the room to the opposite wall. Eddie was safe, Charlie was safe, the baby Alison was safe, I was safe, but Mummy was not.

A large piece of glass was lodged in her back between her shoulder blades. I saw her face, it had gone white, even I as a four year old, realised she was in dreadful pain. I jumped up to pull the offending glass from her back.

"Don't touch it, dear." she said, so calmly you would believe there was nothing wrong, and turning her head she called Charlie from the cupboard. He too was white faced and with a cut on his forehead where a tin of spam had been blown off the shelf and hit him hard. Fortunately, *he was so concerned with his own injury, he did not at first see the glass sticking out of Mummy's back.*

"Come here, dear," she said to him, her voice seemingly soft, almost a whisper.

Wiping off the blood from Charlie's face, she spoke to him as if he was the most grown up boy in England.

"Now, my brave soldier, I want you to go and find Nana she's staying at Auntie Rita's house and tell her to bring the doctor, tell her mummy is hurt. Can you remember that?"

"Yes, mummy,"

"Good Boy, as brave as your Daddy, he will be so proud of you."

We sat silent, watching our Mummy, as she tried to remain motionless during the time it took six year old Charlie to run through that bombed damaged town, to our Auntie Rita's house over a mile away. Rita was one of Mummy's sisters and lived near the station. Then together with Nana, they went to find a doctor and return to us.

That day there was no one about, there were no neighbours about. Phone lines were down and she didn't want Charlie to waste time looking for a neighbour further down the street. She did suggest that if he saw a policeman to ask him to get a doctor, while he went on to Nana's house. Ever practical, she had reasoned that Nana was going to be needed to mind all of us, while she went to the hospital. As it transpired, Charlie ran even as V1's continued to be dropped, for the simple reason he told us later, he passed no one, the streets were deserted, everyone was at work or sheltering and he had no option, no choice left to him, but to run and run.

"Well done, Isobel, well done. You probably saved your Mummy's life by not grabbing at that glass."

The Doctor lifted Alison out of Mummy's arms, which must have been aching, Alison was a bonny baby, Mummy hadn't moved in all of that time. Nana got busy mixing a formula and shooing us all into the back room opposite the kitchen. Seating me beside the unlit fire, she placed the baby bottle in my hands with a, "You feed the baby," and so I did. Watching as Alison sucked speedily on the feeder, I was aware of the

84

brothers playing Snap; they were hidden inside the Morrison shelter that had arrived sometime after Christmas as an alternative to the Anderson shelter. A steel table with wire sides, it was warmer than being outside and at that time, Mummy liked us to sleep in it, because it was quick to access. Ours was wide enough for a double mattress and we would often sleep in there, it seemed as safe as Uncle's billiard table, to our childlike eyes.

Now the siren was again blaring out, and so I got into the Anderson with the baby. But I found she had no intention of going back to sleep. Charlie began tickling her toes and we were chanting in a chorus, 'This little piggy went to market, this little piggy stayed at home, this little piggy had Roast beef, this little piggy had none and this little piggy went... wee, wee, wee all the way home." As we tickled her under her chin, Alison laughed so much that she burped out sick one end and poo from the other, all at the same time. Naturally, I had to clean it up. I was helped by Charlie because I had found the safety pins too difficult to get through all the layers of the terry towelling nappy.

It was the first memory I have of changing a baby's dirty nappy. It reeked as babies nappies do, so I headed off to the kitchen to put it in the bucket under the sink. For a moment I hesitated, there had been no 'All Clear' and all seemed very quiet in the kitchen. So creeping in I was stopped in my tracks by the sight of Mummy's back. It was being cleaned and stitched up with things that looked like large black clips, it was frightening. I quickly dropped the soiled nappy into a bucket and beat a retreat back to the shelter. But the image of Mummy's back was to remain with me all my life.

Soon afterwards, the Doctor took Mummy to the hospital and we did not see her for several days. Nana took over and although already sixty, she was not old in herself, although today trawling through photographs, it is possible to believe she was timeworn rather than ancient. It was something to do with the way she dressed, always with a 'cross over wrap around' pinafore and she permanently did her hair in a top knot.

"She's just not fashionable," I had once heard Mummy saying of her Mother-in-law to a neighbour, as they sat out in the sun, one afternoon following on from another disastrous

night which had left all of us exhausted. It was true, but a bit unfair, for how could she be fashionable with no spare clothing coupons. Nana had always generously given her coupons to Mummy, supposedly for the children, but with Cousin Derek away at boarding in Chailey Craft School in East Sussex and Cousin John being younger and shorter than him; it was at that time, Charlie who had been short of hand-me-downs. I had Angela's; Eddie wore Charlie's and Alison was dressed from a pile of baby clothes crammed into the bottom drawer of the large chest of drawers, which sat behind the bedroom door. Mummy's sisters were all generous to a fault, always handing their children's clothing on to Mummy, the one with a 'quiver' of babies, was how one Aunt expressed it. And sometimes they also shared some of their more glamorous blouses and other clothing with Mummy, for herself.

After the incident with the glass in her back, Daddy, by now somewhere in France had somehow or other contacted our Mother and persuaded her to get us as far away as possible from the V-1 flying bombs, which were increasing in numbers.

"I don't want you to end up like Jack and his Mother!" he had written and he was insistent, we should leave Essex.

He wrote, "The Germans think they're bombing the Houses of Parliament and Churchill has got all the press colluding with him. But, you could be killed, darling, you and the children, you know that, even people in shelters are being killed. You must leave there, and go north."

Yes, Daddy had insisted on us being evacuated, Mummy no longer resisted. She marched all of us down to the Town Hall and up the steps, which in those days stretched right across the front of the highly ornate building, to sign the papers allowing us to be evacuated.

Mummy convinced the man behind the desk that we should be evacuated as a single unit, that following her accident she had no desire to be separated from her children, and he seemed very charming, and sympathetic, 'Don't you worry Mrs Houghton we will get you onto a train somehow.'

Mummy seemed calm and smiling after that, as if she had believed the smiling official, grey faced from months of working indoors, "I promise you Mrs Houghton they will take you, so don't you fret. Now, one more thing; let me check your ration books, please. After looking at our ration books he provided us with travel vouchers, timetables for departure and instructions as to how much we were allowed to take with us, which included our gas masks and two changes of clothes. We were given labels to attach to our coats and we were reminded not to be late."

Isobel stopped speaking.

In the silence that followed I realized that I had been holding myself as if waiting to take a punch right into my stomach. The almost secretive tone Isobel had used as her voice got quieter and quieter with each passing memory spoke louder than you can possibly imagine. I stayed still, hoping the tape had captured the fear that had been in her voice and on her sweet face. I knew she had carried that whole episode in her mind and heart all of her life and I felt so protective of her, that I believed I now understood Gareth's selfless caring attitude towards her. I also now fully understood Mr Williams's reasons for insisting upon this whole episode, as a necessary pathway to understanding the past.

"Enough for today," said Gareth.

Chapter 5

Widening the view point.

I woke early the next morning and lay in the bed thinking about everything I had heard so far, when a knock on the door brought Gareth in with a mug of coffee; it was milky and sweet and accompanied by a plate of thick buttered toast. I sat up in the bed and thanked him.

"Now then young Freddie, I think we should take the morning off. I've ordered Isobel to lie in and she's got breakfast and the paper; the crossword will keep her busy and you and I are going to go out for a walk, while there is some degree of warmth and it isn't raining, because this afternoon the forecast is for a downpour. Your Aunt will be ready to talk to you after lunch okay old chap?"

I thanked him because I knew I needed to get outside and get some fresh air. To my surprise he suggested that we drove into the centre of town and had a look at some of the sites that I perhaps didn't realise were to be important to my study. First off we drove into the centre, past the Philharmonic Hall and down to the bottom of Leece Street. He parked the car in a side street behind what he referred to as St Luke's the bombed out church. And then Gareth and I strolled into the gardens, as he told me that on 5 May 1941 St Luke's was bombed by the Luftwaffe, and that it had been left in the state it was in, as a memorial to all the people who were killed in the bombing raids on Liverpool. We sat together looking up at the stonework of the church, devoid of its roof and all the glass that should have been within the tracery of what were the original windows. The gardens around the church were beautifully laid out with small memorials placed along the pathways. Beyond the railings and the gates there was the noise from Leece Street of endless buses, cars, motorbikes and people hurrying down the hill towards the centre of Liverpool.

For a time we sat in silence and I found that after a while the noise outside the railings seemed to disappear. It was as if the ghosts of the past were all around us and I felt myself breathing more deeply. Turning my head and looking at Gareth who was sitting with his eyes closed the look on his face spoke of peace.

"What are you thinking?" I asked. Even as I said it I felt the crassness of the question. I knew he was remembering all that he had seen of the effects of war, not just here in Liverpool, but in all the places where he had served during his military service.

"Isobel goes on and on about how brave our soldiers were, how they are even now, but I sit here and look at that and I think how brave civilians have to be in times of war. You do realise how important Liverpool was to the whole country?"

I nodded before speaking, "I do know that the docks were important, we visited them officially and our tutor spoke about the fact that during World War II the whole country relied upon them. He said we would have starved if it hadn't been Liverpool, and he told us that his father never saw a banana until he was 10 years of age. I remember him going on about bananas!"

Garth laughed at that, and smiling he said,

"And he was right, Isobel also cracks on about it, she has often said that she was eight before she actually peeled her first banana. You ask her, she thinks it's funny, but apparently she tried to eat the skin, she didn't realise you had to peel it."

"I survive on bananas!"

"You'd have starved!" Gareth laughed, even more heartily. I realized how much I liked this grey hair man, who had only existed in my consciousness as a good looking youngster in an RAF uniform, standing proudly between his parents after his passing out ceremony at Hereford. In service to his country for years, he was an example of loyalty and courage. Eat your heart out James Dean, here was my new hero!

We sat on in peaceful silence for a few more minutes, then as we walked back to the car we left the Memorial Garden by the gate onto Leece Street, and strolled right the way round the exterior of the garden's looking at huge posters attached to the railings. There must been about 24 posters and each one depicted vast bomb damaged areas of Liverpool. The strangest one of all was, according to Gareth, the one taken from Derby Square looking down on a completely flattened area that today is the shopping centre known as Lord Street and the financial area known as Castle Street.

"Trust Queen Victoria not to be blown up," I said, thinking in my juvenile idiocy that that was a *joke he might enjoy, but no, Gareth turned and looked at me, he looked straight into my eyes with the steadiness that made me go very still.*

"Freddie, that statue represents to the people of Liverpool, what the dome of St Paul's did to the people of London. This is an iconic photograph just as important as the one of St Pauls Cathedral against the smoke and fire of the bombing of London. The statue of the old girl represents the courage of Liverpool. Anyone puts graffiti on that, believe you me, the old-timers get very cross. Come, we need to go up to Saint Nicks."

Twenty minutes later, the car parked on a meter, we once again walked into a church garden, this time surrounding the church of St Nicholas. I was beginning to realise how the atmosphere between us changed whenever we walked into a church garden. The noise of the world rushing about beyond the railings seemed to disappear, our pace seemed to slow down and our breathing seemed to relax, as we walked along the side of the building until turning a corner we were confronted by one of the most beautiful statues I have ever seen.

It was as if a spiral staircase was rising up out of the plinth and a little boy was running up it and holding a model aeroplane in his raise hand, while below his mother cared for his sibling. I stood gazing up at it in silence aware that Gareth was watching my face, my reaction to this work of art.

"It's beautiful," I said and then I fell silent once more because words seemed unnecessary, almost as if I would have been stating the obvious. We stood together gazing at the beauty of the statue. Then I felt a hand come down upon my shoulder, a mystery man standing slightly behind me, I had no idea who, and I almost froze until I realised that Gareth had turned his head and was smiling at the stranger.

"So many women and children died in the bombing; many of them while they were hiding under their stairs. All those homes destroyed." The disembodied voice suddenly became a reality as he let go of my shoulder and walked around to stand looking at me with a kindly expression on his face. I noted the dog collar and realised he must be the clergyman attached to this church, naturally he know such specific details. But he looked too young to have lived through it; he was easily 20 years younger than Gareth. As if realising what I was thinking he said,

"Yes, this is my parish, and I often have to show visitors around. I find the Americans and Commonwealth visitors always want to know numbers! Hence I'm learning to be quite good at statistics!" He laughed joyously and Gareth joined in with him.

"The one I know is that over 1000 convoys arrived in Liverpool during the war," said Gareth responding to the friendliness of the priest.

"Have you been into the Exchange Building yet?" he asked Gareth.

"Well I have," Gareth replied, "I'm about to take young Freddie for his first visit."

"I hope you like stairs," was the laughing reply to that, leaving me wondering what it was that was so amusing. I soon found out as we left the churchyard crossing the road to find the entrance to the Western Approaches; the Nerve Centre of the Battle of the Atlantic; preserved almost in its entirety below ground on the road behind St Nicholas's church.

For the next hour Gareth was almost completely silent. As we descended lower to level after level, I lost count of the number of steps we went down, but at each level he let me view the preserved exhibits arranged room by room according to their function, as it had been during the war, and we stood in silence reading the information given.

By the time we got down to the very bottom I was amazed that I had been in Liverpool for more than a year, studying history, and yet I had failed to visit this amazing exibition. When we reached the levels that displayed a shelter and artefacts that people would have had in their own home, it struck me how basic everything was, almost comfortless.

"They had to be tough, a case of sink or swim thank goodness most of them were able to swim. But, for everyone killed, there was someone who was injured, badly injured." Gareth suddenly looked tired, almost grey and I worried for the first time realising how easy it was to forget that he was in fact, seventy!

"I don't know about you Gareth, but I need a coffee, can we get one?" I was changing: I noted

that I was truly concerned for my Uncle and aware that we had to climb back up all those stairs. We got there; I pretended to be tired and climbed slowly, stopping to rest myself on each landing. Garth said nothing, just took the stairs as I did, one flight at a time. Yet it was all an optical illusion, caused by that amazing complex hewn out of the rock that lies beneath so much of Liverpool.

After two hot and sweet coffees, we drove home in a peaceful silence. Isobel had prepared lunch for us: a salad which must have had at least 15 different things in it. I was fascinated; my student idea of a salad was a slice of ham, a lettuce leaf, and two slices of cucumber and if I was lucky quarter of a tomato. But it was a jolly meal and we told Isobel of our tour and our meeting with the priest.

"So, Freddie, you have seen some of the aftermath of war that the people of Liverpool have had to endure. Did you know 75,000 in this one city were left homeless and if you add to that all those in London and Coventry and along the south coast and everywhere else where bomb after bomb destroyed their homes, perhaps you will understand that it wasn't just the time it took to repay the Country's War Debt, that burdened us, it was also the aftermath a long slow rebuilding, when the country was short of wood and bricks, and every other thing needed to put this country back together as we had so much to rebuild. And food was still in short supply; it wasn't until 1953 that food was no longer rationed. I remember seeing Alison and Gareth after they'd been running around in the garden and had rushed in hungry and thirsty, crying their eyes out when mummy quite literally had to tell them she had nothing to give, they had had their slice of bread at teatime and that was that, until the next morning, when she could go shopping again. I think she spent half her time queueing for basic necessities. We all of us went to bed hungry. For us as a family, the aftermath of the war was a long time of real hunger, everyday trying to find food?"

"I hate queueing," I said. I don't know why I said that, but it is true and it somehow registered with me that how we shop today probably was another of those things Isobel calls the aftermath of war. People hate to queue, and yet the real British or is it just the English can't abide queue jumpers. I was chomping away on a mouthful radishes, peppers, and cucumber as these thoughts were churning around in my head. As if he knew what was going on Gareth smiled across at me and said, "Life is very different today!"

I smiled back and said, "It is all part of that thing called the aftermath, thanks Aunt Isobel, I'm going to call my essay The Aftermath!" She looked pleased and said, "Glad to have been of some service young Freddie!"

'I remember the first time I held a lump of real cheese,' Isobel suddenly said as I hacked a piece of Cheddar off the cheeseboard to eat with my crackers.

We spent the next half an hour laughing at ourselves as we challenged our memories to find our earliest food memories.

Isobel claimed it was of a boiled egg and toasted soldiers. Gareth his mother's Corn Beef Hash, when he was about three, and I said, Ice Cream. They both laughed at that, saying that they were hardly surprised, didn't my mother have the biggest freezer in the family.

We adjourned to the sitting room and Isobel renewed her storytelling.

Chapter 6

Evacuees from Essex

"The next day, we left our home, each dressed for travel, with our boxed gas masks over our shoulders and brown luggage labels attached to our coats, in case we got lost, to arrive at King's Cross to find it bustling with people and I remember I felt overwhelmed by the crush of people."

After lunch we had settled down once again in the front room, with the tape recorder whirring away on the small coffee table. Isobel was in fine form and had obviously thought out what she was going to tell me. Again Gareth joined us, and he and I sat in silence as she continued.

"We were shown into a carriage which was meant to be for six persons and because it was a corridor train, it made life easier, at least, so Mummy said. Of course nowadays I realise that was because we had access to the toilet just two carriages along. We settled down, we had one side of the carriage. There were three people sitting opposite us, it became very crowded, and we all saw the reason behind the luggage restrictions. The simple solution was to set us in the luggage rack and put our cases under the seat, on the ground. Charlie, Eddie and I spent the better part of the day sitting curled up on our coats to protect us from the string that made up the bulk of the luggage rack. But it was not without fun, we were able to see out a little bit onto the countryside spread out through the window. We ate a packed lunch of spam sandwiches and had one little hot drink from a flask that Mummy had brought with her. Sensibly she had also brought some small bottles she had saved and washed out before filling them with freshwater. We watched her giving the baby a bottle of cold formula and settling her to sleep in the box like structure that was the carrycot pram, we had brought with us. Fortunately for us the guard of the train was able to put the wheels for the carrycot pram in his van and Mummy could set the carrycot itself on the seat beside her. Every now and then she allowed Charlie down to sit with her because he needed to stretch his legs being six years of age.

When nightfall came we were got down and wrapped up in coats and hats, gloves and scarves before being put back up, this time Charlie and I were able to stretch out and go to sleep in the luggage rack. Our feet often got in the way of *each other until we decided which way we would settle. Strangely enough, for some reason, Eddie was made to sleep down below on the carriage seat, wedged in between the carrycot and Mummy. He was the first one to nod off, he was tired and Mummy was pleased about that: he slept soundly. In fact we all slept quite well because the train was moved into a siding for the night. Later we discovered it was because they were moving military supplies down from the factories and docks in the North, towards the south coast to be transported over to France to support the soldiers who had undertaken the D-Day landings one month earlier.*

It was a hot sunny morning in June, when we woke to discover ourselves still cocooned in the luggage rack, and to find the window of the carriage open and a lady in a uniform, handing in apples and buns and pieces of cheese.

"Hello there, are you Mrs Houghton?"

'Yes I am Mrs Houghton,' said Mummy being excited. 'How do you know my name?'

'Don't you worry Mrs Houghton, we have a list here' and with that she went on to call the names of the other people present in the carriage

as she began giving out food, supposedly as our breakfast

'Sorry you had to spend the night in the siding, but, you know what it's like with the war on, things have to happen elsewhere. You will get to Manchester as soon as possible; you'll be setting off in about half an hour after you've all been given your food.'

I don't remember there being a second night sleeping in the train, but years later Mummy said there were two nights, she maintained that it had been a two day, two night journey on that train. I only remember it as one night, but then I was not yet five, so I believed her version of events.

A bus ride to the school was laid on; it was pandemonium trying to sort out luggage and lost property, but eventually, tired and relieved we arrived at the school that was to be home for the next three days and two nights. Those two nights I remember very well."

I did not want to interrupt her, but Gareth insisted Isobel stopped and we all had a cup of tea. He left the room to go and make it, Isobel shut her eyes, but there was a gentle smile *playing around her mouth. Watching her I realised that she must have been very pretty when she was younger, certainly photographs of her showed a round faced dark haired pretty woman. Suddenly she opened her eyes, and gave me a full smile that spoke of sunshine on a rainy day.*

"Am I doing alright?" Was the surprise question she asked me, as I found myself looking directly at her and realizing once again how alive she was inside of herself.

"You're perfect; I wouldn't want to change a word."

"I've been going to write this for years, but I just never got round to it. There was always something else to do, my life story seemed unimportant."

"I think it's the most important one in all the family. No joke, Auntie, I feel privileged, yes I feel privileged to be the one to hear this."

"Silly boy, it's just about me really."

Looking back, I can well imagine that you think she was displaying a false modesty, but I would not agree with you. Over the years since that day, I have come to realise that there were a lot of heroes in the Houghton family and all of them have a modesty that is quite genuine. Looking at Isobel was like looking at a photograph of my Great, Great Aunt Agnes. Her photograph was on the mantle shelf above Isobel's head, and the similarity was so striking, that I just knew that Agnes and Isobel could be intertwined in their personalities: both were refined, gutsy women, almost uncomplaining, interesting and courageous, and both quaintly old-fashioned in comparison to the modern generation. Neither of them influenced by soap-operas or the Red Top Papers or any silly celebrity culture, their heroes were the men and women who had achieved something useful. Both of them read the Times. Both of them were politically on the right and yet they had strong consciences about the poor of the world. But, perhaps the most significant lesson they had to teach me was the value of family, and caring about each other. Both Agnes and Isobel had followed in the tradition established by Rebecca who as long ago as 1914 had cared for her wounded husband and grieved for her fallen son. I made a note that perhaps I needed to go back into the nether regions of my family history.

I never knew Agnes, but there was something about Isobel which told me, I did know Agnes: I knew what she would be like: and I guessed that if she were sitting here talking to me, she would sound exactly the same as Isobel.

Gareth came back into the room and we set off again within moments of switching on the tape recorder. Isobel was again almost in a trance, as word for word she poured out the next part of her story.

"It was a large dark old-fashioned school obviously built in the 1870s or soon after. It had huge windows everywhere and the hall was enormous with the classrooms off either side of it. And the toilets were outside at the far end of the playground. I hated them, they smelled disgusting. Mummy said, "Just hold your nose and do your business!" She seemed cross and tired and with all the callousness of childhood, I didn't realise her discomfort. Such a dignified and refined woman was my mother. That School Hall was packed with people and we all crowded in and we were told to sit down on the floor, to save the few adult sized chairs for women who were pregnant, and that included our Mummy. Strangely enough she did not look out of place; it

was just that she also had four children as well as the 'one on the way.' Nobody ever said pregnant, it was always 'one on the way.'

Again a lady in a uniform style of coat and hat bustled her way up to Mummy and asked with an imperious voice that was heard throughout the length of the hall

'Are you the Mrs Houghton, insisting upon having a house?'

'Yes, I am,' said Mummy trying not to sound tired, 'and these are all my children. I have been promised a home and I have been promised that we will not be separated from each other.'

'Yes, well there is a slight problem there, Mrs Houghton. At this moment in time, we don't have a house for you, so it is very likely that we will have to separate you.'

'No, no, no! I was promised a house and I was promised I could keep my children with me.'

'Then you just have to stay here until we find one.' She said rather dismissively, I assumed that she had the authority; all I remember is that she seemed very bossy.

'Fine' said Mummy 'and where do we sleep while we are here?'

'On the floor, dear lady, on the floor, do you see that pile of mattresses and blankets over there? Good, commandeer whatever you need, but we've no bed linen.

And so for two nights we slept on hard mattresses placed on the floor, with heavy black smelly blankets over us and pillows without pillowcases. Now we aren't snobs, we never were snobs, but on that day people looked at Mummy as if she was a little bit inflexible because she got handkerchiefs out from her bag and placed them beneath our heads, as we lay on the pillows.

'I don't want my children picking up any germs from those dirty pillows,' is what she said to the rather officious woman, who had told her to select her bedding.

In the end it wasn't too bad and the good point was that as more and more people disappeared, the three of us could run around and play and we played tag and we played hopscotch in the playground. It was a warm and pleasant month and why we know so much about it and remember so much about it, is that one of the *most famous pictures ever taken of us as a group was taken by a Manchester paper and an appeal was put out with it for an empty house large enough to accommodate a family from Essex. Here's that photo; it was kept by Mummy and used by her many years later, as she tried to remember her own history. Even as an old lady of eighty-eight and aphasic because of several strokes, she found the ability to retell yet again the events of that week, of her fear that we would all be separated from her and how stressful the whole period had been for her because her back was still not properly healed and she was in such pain.*

On the third day we were told to pack up all our belongings, transport was coming for us, they had found us a house. As we drove through street after street of back-to-back houses I watched Mummy's face, it was almost rigid with fear. Years later she said when asked what she had felt about being evacuated; she commented on that car journey and said,

'I didn't want us to end in a 'two up two down' with no garden for the children.'

Even to my childish eyes it all looked so different from Essex and everywhere seemed incredibly blackened by soot. But I was relieved when all of a sudden we were out in the countryside and eventually we stopped in what look like a house similar to the one we had come from. It was a terraced house and obviously Victorian in nature. The garden in the front was a long and attractive one. I had enjoyed the car ride from Manchester. It seems strange now that the city has become an enormous conurbation, but back then there were vast tracks of countryside between the various villages and small satellite towns, now part of Manchester. At the time it meant nothing to me that we were being deposited in the centre of a very modest little town called Sale. I do remember the WVS lady who was driving us and how she re-assured us with the news that bombs did not fall in Sale. Charlie questioned her at length about this fact. 'When had the last bomb fallen?' 'How often did they fall?' 'Did they come during the day or the night?'

I was so grateful; I thanked the driver, a WVS lady, as I got out of the car. I remember she commented and said that I was a very polite little girl.

Mummy was smiling until she opened the front door to a house devoid of everything: not so much as a light bulb was available, not a stick of furniture, but it was large and it had fireplaces with beautiful surroundings in the Victorian manner. In the kitchen there was a large blackened old range and in the scullery beyond with a sink and draining board, but otherwise the house was devoid of everything needed, as Mummy wrote to her sister, 'There was not as much as a kettle, and the only privie is outside the back door.'

I remember us sitting on the bare un-carpeted staircase waiting for whatever was going to be delivered for our benefit. It was possibly only an hour's wait but when you're a child, it felt like two hours, and with six-year-old Charlie and three-year-old Eddie I began to get fidgety. Eventually we were allowed out into the front garden, because Mummy could sit on the stairs and look through the open door to keep an eye on us. She was still nervous even though she had moved before. This was her third evacuation to an unknown place. The first in the autumn of

1939, during the phoney war period, when she travelled to Ipswich with Charlie in tow to stay with a family she knew. She had returned home to be with her mother in time for my birth. And then afterwards she was evacuated to a cottage in the grounds of a large estate near Ingatestone, soon after the start of what became known as the Battle of Britain. There she had stayed until all was quiet again, when the bombing was intermittent and because our home now had a garden shelter.

But on the day we arrived in Sale in Cheshire, so far from home and knowing no one in this unfamiliar area, she could be forgiven if sometimes she wished she was back at home. It was hard for her, and mother was grateful when a neighbour appeared with a cup of luke-warm tea, and believe it or not, a cigarette. We left them talking and disappeared out of the front door to examine the long front garden.

That front garden was grassed with long borders down either side and on one side huge laurel bushes, which were able to run underneath, as if they were tunnels. It was quite fun and would became very important to us in the days ahead. Our excitement grew when a small removal type van turned up and two men off-loaded camp beds, director type chairs, a table for the kitchen, together with all the necessities such as cooking utensils. There then followed the hard horse hair mattresses and the basic linen for the house. There was also a box which contained some food.

After the men had left we settled down to some sandwiches and for Mummy, at long last, a hot cup of tea; piping hot as it had been freshly brewed on the newly lit kitchen range. No sooner had we finished that than we set about making up our beds and arranging the chairs at the front room window, where we would sit looking out of the window to see what would happen. Well, nothing did; the road was as quiet as Mother could wish for, and it added to our play area within days.

Charlton Road was a totally residential street in that small town in Cheshire and people were not unfriendly neighbours, very quickly they came forward to introduce themselves, when they realised our predicament. The lady opposite had three boys, and she undertook to look after the three of us while another neighbour set off with Mummy and the baby in the pram to see where the local corner shop was and have a stroll around the immediate vicinity of the house. By the time Mummy returned she was smiling, she felt she had friends around her, and she was delighted that the three boys from the house opposite were reasonably well behaved and had given Charlie, Eddie and myself a happy time playing in the front garden.

That night we all slept well, we were all tired but grateful to be settled. It was quiet and there was no siren all night, and none the next night or the next."

Again the total formality of her description was amazing; equally amazing was how she suddenly stopped. Isobel looked tired and I made the excuse of needing a trip to the bathroom. Gareth announced that he had work to do in the kitchen, together we left her sitting peacefully.

'Get some fresh air, Freddie,' advised Gareth and realising I needed some time to let everything sink in, I gratefully headed off for a run around Sefton Park.

Chapter 7

Gareth

By the time I got back to Isobel she was asleep; well I hoped she was only asleep. She was so very still that it struck me as amazing. Quietly, I left the room pulling the door behind me, making sure it wouldn't wake her and headed off to the kitchen, where Gareth was cooking.

'She's asleep,' I said as I sat down watching Gareth, as he worked. How he manipulated that large knife was fascinating: vegetable after vegetable was shaped into identically sized and lined up beauties.

'That's like a work of art,' I said with real admiration in my voice.

'Chateaux potatoes,' Gareth said with a grin as he put them into water and onto the stove. Then, as he took advantage of my presence to put the kettle on: I relaxed.

'So, how are you getting on, young man? Truthfully now, is any of this going to help you with your essay?'

'She's interesting, if a bit long winded, certainly very detailed. It's almost as if she had the story ready lined up for me. I admit it's very chronological, and maybe that's why she's so able to remember it. I had been worried that she would be boring but she isn't, in fact I am quite fascinated by the details she includes. And the thought of having to arrive into an empty house without any furniture, without any food, with nothing and suddenly the arrival of all this equipment and furniture, I mean who paid for that? Did your mother have to buy it?'

'Not if you mean full market value, no, but it was all part of the government's subsidised Utility range for the victims of the conflict. The government had to do something so many people losing their homes, not just the bricks and mortar everything that was in them. I know we were lucky our furniture survived, but we could not take any of it with us. When you were evacuated you just left with a small suitcase full of clothes, which was all, you were allowed. You locked your front door and just hoped your house would still be there when you got back, if you ever got back. And if the government moved you, it was 'you, a label and a suitcase,' end of story, except Charlie told me he had a pack of cards and his five jacks in his case. Later, as we grew up I found out that there was someone called the air raid distress officer in most towns and cities who was responsible for the distribution of aid, either financial in the form of vouchers or with utility goods. They also were responsible for replacing lost ration books and that in amongst family papers I found a receipt for £25 paid by mother for the contents of the van that had arrived with all those goods. And I looked at the suitcases they had taken with them, I realised that Charlie's suitcase couldn't have held more than one change of clothes and his slippers. Has she shown you the photograph of the group of them?'

'Yes, yes she is very proud of it.'

'Well, of course I don't remember anything, I'm there, but unseen, as you realise. I'm the product of a flying visit by my father, saying goodbye before leaving for Europe, and leaving her pregnant yet again. I suppose I'm grateful for that, I wouldn't be here if it hadn't been for D-Day! He went over D-Day minus 6 or was it plus 6; I can't quite remember, but Isobel will. You know he never talked about it, until the last year of his life. That's the soldier's way isn't it?'

I looked across the table at him silently playing with his empty coffee mug. Gareth Houghton had to be 70 years of age, he had been born in 1945; yet even I could see that he looked years younger, and he looked fit. I suppose that wasn't surprising, seeing as he was still a regular tennis player. 'Only play with the vets now!' Was his way of describing his fitness regime, 'Try and play at least twice a week,' was his reply when asked how often he played.

'Of course, I take after our mother's side of the family, the Bedford's, whereas, Isobel is undoubtedly a Houghton. She has brown eyes and I have blue.'

I laughed at that, but I didn't like to say to him, that he had a longer and leaner face than his sister, because that too was an obvious family characteristic.

My Grandmother Alison also had the blue eyes and light brown hair that must have once been Gareth's colour. Now his hair was almost cut to his skull in the way military people keep their hair very short. In the silence I smiled to myself as I realised that my father Raymond had similar colouring to Gareth, and that seeing both men, I now had a two-stage impression of what I would look like in the future, at fifty like my father and hopefully by seventy, like Gareth: it was all so uncanny it made me shiver. My father Raymond was not as tall as Gareth, so I was hopeful that as I was still growing; I might one day be as tall as Gareth, rather than squat like my father. I laughed at myself inside as I realised I was being silly, I was already 3 inches taller than my father and I suddenly and silently thanked God for that. But then dad wasn't that squat, I was being mean. I just wanted to be as tall as Gareth.

It was a comfortable silence; I felt it was a manly silence that seemed almost to surround us with a secure understanding of who we were, of what we were. Suddenly I had a great desire to tell Gareth that that is what I wished I had with my father.

'Did you get on with your father?' I asked him in a quiet, and I hoped respectful voice.

'I suppose I should say yes and no. I only knew him as the product of the war. He came back with shellshock and according to my mother, a man so changed that she found life very difficult. And if Charlie and Isobel are to be believed, they also had a difficult relationship with the man who came home. I suppose today they would diagnose it as Post Traumatic Stress Disorder or syndrome, or some such condition.'

A look came over Gareth's handsome face which said that like his father he had suppressed his real feelings.

'So he was difficult?'

'With me, well I was four or five before I can say I experienced any of his reactions to life. But he was an irascible man, all my life that I have any memory of him, a rigid time keeper, sometimes it was difficult to remember the fourth commandment. Again you best ask Isobel.'

He paused for a moment and in silence he looked across the table at me and his incredibly blue eyes focused on my face in such a way that I felt sad for him. It was a wordless moment that spoke volumes of unexpressed events in his young life that even now all these years later there was still a painful reaction attached to those thoughts and memories. When he next spoke he changed the subject matter in such a way that I was surprised and yet moved by his consideration.

'Sorry Freddie, I should have asked, is your room okay?'

'Oh, yes thanks! It's considerably better than my university digs.'

'And why is that? I know you're in digs with other students. Is it all rotten furniture or are they just messy and never washing up after themselves?'

'I'm afraid so. Washing up is a pain! I don't like washing up, but fortunately we do have a dishwasher and some really pretty girls who stand around it chatting as they fill it and empty it almost daily. But with eight of us sharing, it's cheap and cheerful and it's the company that keeps me there. We have a really good laugh, Uncle, not joking. Luckily none of us is a smoker!'

'That's definitely a help.'

His voice seemed changed and for a moment I felt the discipline of the military in his tone. He was looking directly at me, don't ask me why, but, I froze.

'I'm glad to hear that young man. You won't last long if you get into cigarettes and drugs and beer and God knows what else. Take my advice and avoid all that.'

Fortunately, I realised that he was just being kind in his warning. Although he knew who I was and where I came from, I felt the need to reassure him.

'Well I was lucky I grew up in a household where there are never any cigarettes; dad's only weakness is probably his fondness for wine with his dinner.'

Gareth described my father as a surgeon who has to 'man' up to his job, ending with the comment, "He can't afford the shakes!"

'Yeah, he's healthy!' Said I with possibly a note of boredom.

'When I was your age everyone smoked, everywhere, it was disgusting, really it was. During the war, which is what I believe you're here to talk about, it was the tranquillizing drug of choice, as people faced the fear of it all. I suppose they just had the attitude eat, drink, and smoke, do what you like, because tomorrow you might die. And world-wide fifty five million of them did!'

'Have you ever been to war, Uncle?'

'Hey, less of the Uncle!

'Sorry, Gareth. But did you go to war?'

'Yes, but only for a year. I was out in Aden in the 60s. That's a forgotten war, if ever there was one, ranks alongside the Korean War, have you heard of that one?'

'No, neither!'

'Falklands, Bosnia, anywhere? I thought you did A level history!'

'I did the Henry's!'

'So, I suppose you can give me a blow by blow account of Agincourt? I thought so! Dear God, modern education! You do realise that Matt's father, Peter was in the RAF and that both of Rob's parents were also out at Camp Bastion?'

'Yes, and mine too, dad was a bit of a hero at the hospital out there.'

'In point of fact, did you know that your Great, Great Grand Uncle Henry, drowned while in the Royal Navy during the First World War? Get Isobel talking about that one, because by George *that had disastrous consequences for our family, and his other brother who was killed later in 1944 at Arnhem! You can go and see his grave; Isobel's been over there to see it. What about your mother's family? I believe you've got a second cousin who was fighting in Northern Ireland, who committed suicide, and your Aunt Sally hates talking about it. Now there's a cause and effect you could investigate.'*

I looked across the table and could see that there was somehow or other an excitement within him, as he spoke. It was as if the pride he had in those who had fought and died was a reality that he treasured. I hesitated for a few moments, I let the silence hang between us as I tried to think, 'what should I ask, what should I say?'

'I do know that Isobel's husband was also in Aden, is that where he was injured.' I tentatively asked,

'You will have to stay here a month if you want her to rabbit on and on and on about her precious Brian. I just don't listen to her any more. The latest thing is, if only he'd been injured in Afghanistan! The hospital at Camp Bastion was apparently the be all and end all of hospitals, and

not just because your father had been out there as a surgeon. She is way off beam because Brian would have been just as badly off now as then. When you are shot you are shot, when you are blasted you are blasted, when you're crushed you are crushed. That's war!'

Wow, some outburst! I sat very still, waiting to see what he would say next.

But Gareth seemed to calm down again and I breathed a sigh of relief. So here was a major lasting conflict between the two of them. A consequence to follow and write about: I suddenly realized that I was not going to waste my time here in this quaintly old-fashioned household, there were so many layers of real history, real memories that I could see myself writing more than one essay.

'I have to ask, Gareth, if you don't mind, why did you chose to be so long in the RAF. Dad calls you a long serviceman, that's how he said it, 'Oh yes, Gareth was a long service man!' I mean that seemed odd to me. What does 'long' mean?'

'The difference between doing National Service and signing up as a Regular, that's all. Well, in my case, I signed up for a twenty-five year

stint. Charlie was already in as such, so I followed suit. I don't regret it, never have done.'

'And you miss it now?'

'Yes and no. I lived with men who became wonderful friends and the sport was important to me as a means of keeping fit. Funny really, it's only when it's over that you realize that there is a sense of belonging that, yes, you can kick against it, but it's looking back I have come to appreciate that it also cushions you from some of life's harsher realities. Like a roof over your head! Like food on the table! And there's always something to wear?'

Gareth suddenly laughed, and I joined in, because I think I understood. The difference between college and home was the same, always a roof over my head always food on the table and always clean clothes to wear. I couldn't help myself as I responded with,

'Sounds a bit like a family!'

'A great many lonely people say that about their jobs, so why not?'

'But, you were a chef!'

'Does that bother you? Even if I'd wanted to fly they wouldn't let me; I hadn't got the eyesight for it. I was fifteen and a half when I joined up. When you live in a large family, Freddie, the one thing you learn is how to cook. And cook I could, so there I was as a trainee catering officer: but I had skill already so I was very quick to go up the ranks, as high as I could without actually being an officer. I didn't want to be an officer: not that I didn't mix with them several times when I was out on the tennis court, or badminton court or any other court for that matter, partnering up in the various tournaments. That's how the commander got wind of me and kept me at home, as you might say, here in England. Listen it wasn't altogether a cushy life, it was quite hard at times, especially when I had to cook for all the important visitors who turned up; and I had quite a few bossy commandant's wives to contend with, but mostly I enjoyed it all and they didn't exactly overwork me, except on the monthly dinner party for various bigwigs! And then there was the occasional Royal visitor!"

"You cooked with the Queen?"

"Ah, now if I answer you, I'll have to shoot you! I am still under the Official Secrets Act, don't you know?"

"Now you're teasing me!"

"Am I? Don't think so, Freddie."

"Well then try this one did you ever shoot anyone when you were out in that place?"

"Aden? No, I was cooking! And boy was it hot!"

"But Isobel's husband, he was fighting?"

"Yes and a sniper got him in the back."

By now he was ready to carry on with his cooking, so with a nod of his head he sent me on my way back to Isobel, and as I left the kitchen he handed me a cup of tea to take to her.

Chapter 8

Reviewing the situation

It was almost impossible to sleep, late autumn winds were blowing fiercely outside the house and inside it was my brain that was storming against every thought of sleep, there was too much in my head! In the end I put the tape recorder on and listened to Isobel's commentary of her first day at school.

In my mind I was comparing it to my own memories of being five, of being dressed in a maroon and grey school uniform with the maroon shade to the four quartered grey and maroon skullcap. For me my first day at school, had all been about the uniform. For Isobel it was to become the nightmare that would never leave her. Strangely enough I had always known about Isobel's problem. Both my parents had at various times told me not to comment whenever we had received a letter or card which demonstrated her inability to spell properly. It was almost a joke in private but never in public.

She had spoken at length on the tape about how happy she had been at the thought of going to school, especially as with the quietness of the *neighbourhood, her mother had believed it possible for Charlie to walk his sister into her new school and introduce her to her class teacher: apparently that had all felt very grown up. Every minute detail of that day was recorded on the tape: especially the information that it was when small slates and pieces of chalk were given out for a drawing class, that once again the fear and dread of Hitler was forced onto her consciousness. Hearing about it directly from her I felt her fear is a reality. I have read elsewhere that being left-handed was regarded as wrong in those days. And when she had picked up the chalk to begin drawing on her little board, she was cut short by the teacher's alarming use of a wooden pencil case to slam down onto her hand and send the chalk flying.*

But it was the words that accompanied that action which have upset her to this very day, for the teacher had said,

'What are you Hitler's child?'

Even as she said it all these years later, Isobel went as white as white could be, and her hands formed fists as if she wanted to punch someone. The next moment she was crying, and I had switched the tape off and let her cry.

It was in that moment that I felt truly gauche and stupid, unable to put my arm around her to comfort her, unable to think of any word that would help take away the obvious pain of that moment. Fortunately Gareth had come into the room and seeing the state of her, he simply asked,

'First day at school?'

"Yes, I have upset her, I'm sorry.'

There was silence for a moment, and then Gareth suggested that I asked her exactly what happened next. He said, if I kept talking to her she would calm down and begin to express how she truly felt.

'Did it hurt you very much?' I queried and as I did so, I put my arm across her shoulders and pulled her slightly towards me. It seemed to have the effect that Gareth had suggested and she calmed down. Turning her face towards me; now only inches from my face, she tearfully whispered, 'She could have called me anything, but not Hitler's child. You must know what Hitler meant to me; the man who'd killed Uncle Jack and the baby, the man who had blitzed our home and injured mother. It was the cruellest name in the world, I was four, a trusting child who became terrified that it was true and I really was Hitler's child. Please don't laugh; my hand was hurting, but my heart was even sadder, could I possibly be related to that evil monster?'

It was an extraordinary moment, but it gave me food for thought, one of the things that I thought of as a possible career was to be a teacher. Was it possible that a teacher could affect the whole of the child's life just by one nasty comment?

It was Gareth who spoke next as he said 'It was almost universal in those days children were not allowed to be left handed. Poor Issy, she went through weeks of being smacked, of having her left hand tied behind her back, and of the public humiliation of never getting spelling right during the old-fashioned spelling bees that were daily occurrences at that school. Later she was labelled word blind, a late developer, a slow learner and numerous other comments which frequently suggested that she was mentally lazy.'

At this point I almost angrily interjected 'But she is a writer, look at all the things she has written.'

'Yes, but everything is edited by friends or family, and in some cases by paid editors.'

Turning the tape on again I listened into Isobel describing what she called her failures: the 11+, five attempts at O Level English, unable to get into university, no degree, just a qualification to teach needlework.

'But you were brilliant at needlework, Auntie.' I said with enthusiasm. 'I only have to look around this house to see your needlework everywhere: your beautiful embroidery, never mind the curtains and the cushions. And what about that gorgeous patchwork quilt on my bed upstairs, come on now, it's absolutely beautiful and must be worth a small fortune.'

Both Gareth and Isobel had laughed at me as Isobel beamed as she said, 'It was Rebecca who taught me to sew.'

Up until that point very little had been said about Rebecca, the second wife of John Houghton, Isobel and Gareth's Grandfather who had been born in 1860. He had died in 1931, and few people in the family spoke of him now. Rebecca, his second wife, had followed Anne and the children north to help Anne with Gareth's birth. She was a midwife, and it was a known fact that she had assisted at the birth of Charlie, Isobel, Eddie and Alison. When eventually Isobel was able to explain what had happened at school, it was Nana Rebecca who saw a solution to the problem.

I loved the way Isobel explained what had happened. 'Well, I wouldn't eat my tea, and when mummy told me off for wasting food, I told her I couldn't because I mustn't use the fork in my left hand. There was a lot of argument, but I had persisted and I explained how the teacher had said I must not use my left hand. Eventually I told her what had happened, all of it and Nana sitting there listening said, 'Didn't she tell you about sewing?' When I said no, all the teacher had said was that I must never use my left hand and then she had tied my hand behind my back.

But Nana laughed and laughed and laughed and said,

'Don't worry Izzy I'll show you what you have to do with your left hand.'

Nana got out mother's sewing basket and she took out the darning mushroom. Putting the darning mushroom inside a sock and pulling it down tight, so that the open hole was on the top of the mushroom, she then threaded a large needle with thick wool and she came and sat behind me. Bringing her arms over the top she took my left hand and she made me grip the sock onto the mushroom. 'Never let go of the mushroom,' she had said, 'your left hand is always there to hold your sewing, your left hand is the holding hand, not the writing hand. The right hand is the writing hand, the sewing hand, the knife hand and the drawing hand. She was very silly not to tell you.'

Isobel carried on explaining, 'It all made sense to me and before I was six I was one of the best needle-woman in the family. Every night I darned all the socks, I learnt to sew on buttons, I learned to patch and I was the pride and joy of my mother and Grandmother when I hand stitched mother's Christmas present for 1946. It was a silk cami-knickers made out of a piece of discarded parachute silk.'

She had listed on the tape all her sewing skills: French seams, open seams, something called a placket, a scalloped hem, and a hand worked buttonhole, which she described as perfectly proportioned for the white button she had pinched from the front of her own liberty bodice.

Again it was Gareth who carried on as Isobel seemed to sink back into her armchair in total contentment at the memory of her childhood achievements.

'So now you know why your Aunt dictates her writing, all her life she has been bugged with the disappointment of not being able to spell sufficiently correctly to be considered a creative writer.'

'But look at her now!' I queried and for a few moments he looked back at me in silence before saying,

'Yes, we are all proud of her now, but she went through hell as she was growing up. She thanks the nuns who taught her: apparently they were exceptionally patient with her difficulties. And she was lucky; her needlework skill was so good it made her stand out from all the others. Father would never let her even dream of being a writer. Every attempt she made to find time to write, he somehow or other seemed to block the possibility.'

Pausing for a moment, he looked across at Isobel and said to her,

'Tell Freddie about the children's nursery and you being lost.'

Chapter 9

'An unknown child from a London bomb site'

Now I really was intrigued by Gareth's comment. I looked from one to the other, the question must have been written on my face, for this was something I had never heard mentioned by any of the older members of the family.

I took a moment to change the tape, putting a fresh cassette in and turning I looked at Isobel and asked, 'Ready?' She smiled and seemed incredibly relaxed and she said, 'Yes, I would like to tell you about that.' For the next half hour Gareth and I listened in silence to the old lady who seemed to be in another world. She did not look at us, and she did not hesitate, as she told us of this incident in her life.

'Because Nana was 60, the authorities would not allow her to look after all four of us, so Eddie, Alison and I were put into an orphanage when the time came for Gareth to be born. Equally they would not allow Nana to be the midwife. Now there were few doctors around and so mummy had to go to a so-called nursing home, it was in fact a small local hospital that was full of women about to give birth. There was one midwife to care for dozens of women: altogether there were about 100 women in various stages of pregnancy and motherhood at that place. There were no other members of staff, mother had to report two weeks early, and during that period all the women waiting to give birth would do the cooking and cleaning and laundry for those who had had their baby's already. Then it was the practice in those days that once the woman had given birth she had to lie in for the next two weeks.

Meanwhile in another part of Cheshire, Eddie, Alison and I, were being cared for in an overcrowded orphanage. The cots and beds were quite literally cheek by jowl, and we could climb over the sides of the cots. There were fewer people to look after us, we more or less had to take care of ourselves, and I took charge of Eddie and Alison. The trouble came when measles was brought into the place by a newcomer who coughed and sneezed all over us. I was one of the first to catch first the cold and then the disease. Then I was taken in an ambulance to a hospital, the file with my details in it was placed on the stretcher upon which I was lying, together with the file for the other girl on the second stretcher.

We came to a hospital; she was taken in with one of the files.

Whatever you should hear from any of the others about what happened next; I can only say what I remember. We drove on, I must have fallen asleep because I have no idea how far we went. The upshot of it was that I ended up in the hospital and I clearly remember being examined and x-rayed before being put to bed in a four bedded room. There were no other patients, so it seemed frighteningly quiet and when the nurses came in and out they were all of them covered in white, with white masks over their faces. I remember people fussing over me, one young nurse in particular seem to have been told to take care of me. Days went by, I can't tell you very much about it, I was very ill. When I began to get better, I realised that I had been there some time and I began to worry about what was happening with my mother and the new baby. Also I couldn't understand why no one had been to see me. I could not hear what was being said to me, and I could not speak.

When as a teenager I question my parents about the whole incident, I was told, that I had become lost to them, missing: because when the whole search was over, it was realised that I had been given the wrong file at the first hospital the ambulance had stopped at, and I had consequently been registered as an 'unknown child from a London bomb site,' now it made no difference to me at that time, but it had a near disastrous effect upon mother. After Gareth was born, she had her two weeks of lying in and resting and then she returned home and rang the orphanage to enquire about us.

It was then that she learnt that I had been moved to a hospital, because I had measles and diphtheria. If I remember correctly she was advised to wait another week until I would be completely clear of the disease and not infect the others. But when the time came and she went to collect me, she was presented with the girl who was similar in age and size, but who certainly was not her daughter. To her dying day, mother said it was one of the worst days of her life and she feared the worst. I cannot tell you the details but somehow or other upon hearing what had happened, Daddy went AWOL and set off from Poland, where he was at that time one of the British intelligence officials entering the Bergen-Belsen concentration camp.

Before he had arrived home, his commanding officer had been in touch with mother and settled that daddy would not be Court Martialled for being absent without leave: he reduced the affair to 'compassionate' leave.

And so daddy arrived at the Cheshire house and was told not to be frightened, he was no longer a suspect on an AWOL charge. Various things made life difficult as they went searching for me. At that time with the shortage of petrol, you were not allowed to travel more than 30 miles without a permit. So first off, with the help of the orphanage they rang different hospitals; no one had any evidence of Isobel Houghton.

Then as the news spread around the village, help was given in the form of some 'spare' petrol and daddy was able to motorbike further afield looking for me. He went from one hospital to another with no success.

Later I was told it was the idea of one of the neighbours, that a photograph of me should be put in the local papers. After this was done, there was a gap of a few days, because of paper shortages, most local papers were only printed once a week, nevertheless, as they came out, both *mummy and daddy began to feel hopeful that they would find me eventually. And they did, because the young nurse, who had been looking after me, in the old Chester Infirmary, recognised me and spoke to the matron, who in turn contacted the police.*

What I do remember is daddy walking in to that room, I was sitting up in bed, still very silent because of the stress that had been placed upon me with the diphtheria, and yet I remember as clear as anything I managed to say, 'Daddy, daddy.' And I remember I cried and cried.

Back at the house there was great rejoicing and I remember neighbours coming in to bring little food gifts, so that we had quite a boisterous party. I know there was jelly, because that was about all I could eat.

That's when I met Gareth for the first time. He was quite sickly, and had begun to lose weight far too fast for the doctor and Nana not to be worried.

I had to spend a few more days in bed, and I had the great joy of being cared for by my Auntie Agnes who turned up on leave. She was serving as a Wren and worked in a busy office as a typist.

None of us had any idea just how much that illness was to cause me trouble in the coming years. First off, penicillin was still relatively new, and I was given an excessive amount by today's standards: but how can we complain for it saved my life. The effect on my throat and ears was very marked and for the next two years I had difficulty hearing. This led to a situation where mother and I developed our own simple sign language: it affected my early schooling, and I had considerable difficulty with teachers who did not understand that I could not hear the difference between certain sounds. On my seventh birthday, there was the spelling B and I was asked to spell a word: I heard the word 'inplicit' when the teacher had actually said 'implicit' and she believed I was being difficult. There's no need to recount the barney that followed, but the next day mother was summoned and after listening to the raised voices and the quite harsh comments, I so remember my mother pleading that I was a slow learner and could the teacher not be patient with me. Mother explained that we often communicated with signs that we had invented ourselves, and it was that teacher who suggested that mother sent me for speech therapy. Instead of speech therapy, I was sent for elocution lessons, for which mother paid, and for which I am eternally grateful, because I have frequently earned my keep by use of my speaking voice.

So, you see Freddie, I ended the war able to sew, learning to knit and although deaf at the time the war actually ended, within months that became a case of just being hard of hearing. And because of that having elocution lessons, which gave me the other career I love, acting.

I switched off the tape and smiled at her. 'I'm so glad to hear you say that,' I said to her, 'I've always wondered where your Essex accent had got to.' Gareth began to tease me, 'Speaking of accents young man, I can hear a wee bit of scouse creeping in there!'

Laughing at that, I looked back at Isobel realising that she had gone strangely quiet. It was as if something important was being turned over inside her head. I waited; at last I had learnt that sometimes it was better to say nothing, and to give people time to find the words they wanted to use to tell their story.

In the silence, Gareth fidgeted for a moment and then settled back into his armchair, his eyes fixed upon his sister. I saw affection *there, and also I recognised, that like myself, he realised she needed time to formulate her next memory into words that would have meaning for all of us.* 'We had a VE day street party, like nothing you could imagine when you see photographs in the press. From the top end of the road to the bottom table after table was brought out from the houses and sheds of every building in the road. If there weren't enough actual tables, then I remember seeing boxes and empty barrels being used to support doors that had been taken from their hinges. Everything was covered with sheets and old curtains. People had been saving for that party for months, once they realised that the possibility of victory was there. Mummy found a second-hand frock in blue-and-white and she sewed on red Ric-Rac braid around the collar, sleeves, and the hem. I know I felt very patriotic and I had red white and blue ribbons in my hair. Somehow or other colourful bunting appeared as from nowhere, the street was festooned from side to side and along the front of the houses. It was noisy with music, radios were turned towards open windows and happy patriotic music was being played to help everyone enjoy their parties all over the country.*

I remember the moment when a man's voice announced some sort of countdown to the end of hostilities. All that Mummy said on that day was, 'No more bombs, we are safe now, thank God.'

The war was over, as far as we were concerned. We packed up and went back to Essex, where sometime later we went to a VJ party.

I was old enough to know what was going on: for us the aftermath of war was eight long years of rationing, of mother's endless endurance of a shell-shocked de-mobbed husband who eventually came home more violent and angry than you can ever imagine, and a housing situation that today still haunts many of my generation.'

We sat on in silence, and then Gareth made a sign which said, enough for today. I began to pack up my tape recorder, and even before we had left the room, Isobel was asleep in her chair.

Gareth and I made our way to the kitchen were with a coffee in front of me, we sat in silence, until he said,

'Well, have you enough now, do you need more?'

'She's opened a can of worms!' I replied, even as a shiver went down my spine, I knew that I had heard no more than the beginning of the story, it was the expression on her face which spoke louder than actual words: Her memories of the post war period still rankled with Isobel.

Chapter 10

When Freddie begins to broaden his thinking after meeting a man called Bert.

Gareth obviously felt sorry for young Freddie, and decided that the lad needed a break away from the old lady. So having settled her for an early night, the two of them headed off into town and found themselves with a pint of the best in front of them, as they settled into a corner of the Philharmonic pub on Hope Street.

'Do all old people spend their time just thinking about the past?' queried Freddie.

'I suppose it's the difference between happy and sad memories, in relation to feelings of worthlessness, of being ignored by the world, feeling that you've given so much and yet got so little back in return. Who wants to notice us? A feeling of being dumped on the scrap heap of life, useless, obsolete, unwanted, is not a very healthy attitude, but I suppose it is inevitable in the case of some!'

As if ashamed of himself, Freddie could not bring himself to look directly at Gareth, as he thought about this comment. Deep inside he realised that he was one of those people who really had no concern for the thoughts and feelings of old people, and yet he was studying history for what: what did he intend to do with this in-depth looking at the past? Taking a sip of his beer, his face still turned away from his Uncle, and looking around at the people sitting about, he suddenly found himself speculating upon their possible lifetime scenarios. He looked at one man, who must have been well over 80 years of age, tucked silently into a corner, his eyes looking down at his hands as he rubbed them in the way that people with arthritic hands do. Freddie looked up at his Uncle said,

'Look at that man over there; he must have been in the war, what do you suppose his story is?'

'You want to ask him?'

'I can't do that, he might not want to speak to me and... and he would be embarrassed.'

'Would he? I don't think he would mind, most old people love it if someone speaks to them. Follow me young man.' And with that Gareth stood up and picking up his drink headed across the pub and sat down beside the old man in the corner.

'Hello Sir, do you mind if we sit and chat with you, my nephew here is studying at the University and has to write an essay about what we did during World War II, here in Liverpool. Could I possibly ask you, do you have any memories of that time that you could share with him?'

Freddie held his breath as he sat down opposite the old man, and smiled as he held his hand out to shake hands in a gesture of politeness. Gareth noted and smiled. This nephew was not so bad after all.

'I were a Docker during that time lad that I were and it were dirty work, and we worked every hour the good Lord gave us. We 'ad to turn the ships round quick like, afore them Gerry's could bomb them.'

Fascinated by the Scouse accent coming from the old man, Freddie was momentarily stunned into silence, but his eyes never left the old man's face. Gareth could see what was going on and so he took over for a few moments.

'My name is Gareth and this is my nephew Freddie, he's from down south'

'Bert, me name's Bert, nice to meet yer and what does the lad need to know?

Encouraged by the very pleasantness of the old man, Freddie suddenly sat up straighter and smiles as he said,

'We went to see the Battle of the Atlantic control centre. Did they control the docks?'

'Oh, I sees what you mean, well, they controlled, no I suppose you would say, organised the dock management, each dock 'ad its own management, the control centre, the ships in and out, hopefully without them bumping into each other, I mean, there never will be another time when so many ships would head into Liverpool. Then it were as if the Mersey were full of ships and boats of every size and shape. You'll not see the like ever again. You know lad, a convoy could arrive with hundreds of ships in it, and we had to empty them, day or night. Sometimes we worked in the dark. You have to realise England, were, no, not just England, Scotland and Wales as well, were under siege from the U-boats. Now they were the things we feared because every boat lost were like losing a whole army of 40 foot trucks, loaded with supplies. You know lad, you go on that there motorway, and you see lorry after lorry heading to and from the docks, one ship could fill up two dozen of them with food, aye food and then there were the weapons, sometimes with coal. We worked over time, especially when the bits for the re-pairing of the planes arrived, all coming off them there ships and them Gerry's never gave up, they tried to bomb and bomb the docks. Trouble is at the time, when they missed the docks they hit the town; they were always bombing the top of the hill they flattened all round Derby Square all the way down across the town.' The old man paused, and he seemed to be struggling for breath, and then suddenly Bert asked Gareth.

'As he seen the photographs?'

'Yes, he's seen quite a few of them now.'

'Aye, then you has some idea how much they wanted to flatten the docks. You see lad, they wanted to starve us into submission. An' we were never gonna give in, no lad, not our Liverpool Dockers, toughest bred in the world that we were. An' thank God for Canada and the commonwealth, that's what I say!'

Bert took a sip of his beer, the glass was now nearly empty, so Gareth asked him if he'd like another, at which Bert smiled happily and Gareth went off to refill all three of the glasses. In the silence Bert looked across at Freddie and smiling as if he was happily looking at his own Grandson, Bert realised that the younger man was still slightly embarrassed to speak to a stranger. Freddie was a southerner, a foreigner to Bert's generation.

'You at the Uni, then, young Freddie?'

'Yes, I'm in my second year, reading history, but thinking of doing a year of politics.'

'Nice to have a choice lad, we had no choice, left school at 14 straight down the docks, at first I were just sweeping and fetching stuff in and out of the warehouses. You got very dirty, I'd get home and I couldn't even have a decent bath, me mam had painted a black line around the bath, yeah, a black line with paint, it were just 2 inches up and that's all you got 2 inches of water, there were nought you could do about it: there were no fuel to heat hot water. Me mam used to *say if King George had a line of paint round his bath, then we had to do the same. I found it easier to boil up the kettle and just stand at the sink and wash meself down. And if it weren't the state of me neck and ears, to annoy her, she'd go mad because me clothes were like full of dirty black soot, oh aye they could almost stand up on their own, an' when I were travelling home on the dock railway, I realised all of us men and boys alike stank to high heaven of a dirty smokiness that went everywhere with us. You could tell if a man were a Docker the dirt were like a badge of honour. It were nearly as dirty as being a Bevan boy, there weren't much difference between us.'*

By now Gareth was sitting down having sorted the drinks and leaning back, he left Bert and Freddie to keep the conversation going. He sensed that if he stayed out of it, Bert would gradually draw Freddie into asking those questions that he needed to ask.

The drink was going down well, Freddie was asking question after question, mostly about what the goods were, what sort of food did they have coming in, what sort of raw materials for industry. Gareth listening in, realised what the boy was getting at when he suddenly veered away to the topic of rationing when he said,

'But, Bert, I mean wasn't there a lot of black-market stuff, you know didn't they call them spivs? I heard that they would steal things from the warehouses.'

'Well if there were, lad, I never saw them and I never got anything to sell meself, me mum would have loved a pair of silk stockings, I can tell yer.'

Gareth watched Freddie growing more and more relaxed as he chatted with Bert. It pleased Gareth to see the young man behaving with such gracious courteousness, and he wished Freddie's parents were here to see it.

Ray, and Sally his wife, were known to have been disappointed in their son, well at least Surgeon Commander Raymond Woods, was at every family gathering pontificating upon the frustration he felt with regards to his only child. He was jealous of the wonderful Matt and Robert, both of whom had excellent school results, A+ in everything, useful degrees under their belts, and fully employed within useful industries. But his son had shown no inclination to aspire to be useful or hope for a rewarding career sometime in the future.

Sally was also disappointed, but mainly because she could not boast about any of his achievements, he didn't even excel in sporting ventures. She hated the feeling that her sister Jenny, who had been married to Ray's second or third cousin, who was also a military man, and who had died in Bosnia during the conflicts, was merely being polite whenever Sally tried to comment upon Freddie's kindness to animals, yes that was all she could think of in praise of her son.

It was equally disconcerting for Freddie that his parents did not understand him. The feeling that he stood apart from the rest of the human race had been his bug-bear throughout his teenage years. It had seemed to Freddie that nobody understood him, and his usual method for soothing his troubled spirit was to withdraw to his bedroom, needing to be alone, and to spend hours playing computer games. If he read one book a year that was a miracle, according to his mother; and here he was finding himself now living as a second-year student researching a topic that he was beginning to find very interesting. It still bugged him somewhat as to why his tutor had selected the subject matter, when it was Freddie's opinion that history happened hundreds of years ago and what was happening today was not relevant to history. If you want history you had to go back into the past. That was very much his attitude, and he had voiced it on many occasions even while supposedly studying British and European history of the 21st-century.Gareth watched and felt he was seeing a sea-change of opinion taking place before him.

The evening came to an end with the promise to meet up again the following week.

'I'll be wanting to hear lad, how yer getting on.'

With his usual graciousness, Gareth offered the old man a lift, and that was how they discovered that Bert lived in a 'two up two down' house on Back Saint Catherine Street.

Freddie was silent the rest of the way home and finding that Isobel was already in bed and asleep the two men quietly went off to their rooms to settle for the night.

Immediately he had shut his door, Freddie felt that he could not sleep; Bert had taken his mind into a wider view of what war meant.

Getting out his laptop he immediately googled Bevan Boy before he began researching the bombing of Liverpool during the Second World War.

Using his tape recorder, to keep all the details down clearly, knowing that he would want to include them in his final essay, he worked away for the next two hours, examining question after question that sprung into his mind, and recording the positive results he gained from the world wide web. The magic of the Web was with him that night, never again to be marginalised by the constant use of computerised games: it was as if his brain had been woken up and needed feeding with information.

By the time he was ready for bed and sleep, his brain was almost overloaded. He was particularly interested in details such as the fact that there were 11 miles of dock side quays, and that over a thousand convoys, many with several hundred ships in them, arrived at the port of Liverpool. The truth was there, Bert had not lied, the people of Britain would have starved but for Liverpool. By the end of the war the city was left with 90,000 homes destroyed, and several thousand people killed. On eight nights alone in May 1941 the Luftwaffe killed 1746 people, and injured a further 1154. His mind raced through a myriad of ideas for his final essay. Detail; truthful detail was what he needed, and there it was: beginning with the detail of St Luke's bombed on the 5th of May 1941. And even earlier 28th of November 1940 the air raid shelter on Durning Road which took a direct hit killing 166 people, mostly women and children.

Yes, Bert had put an almost clinical account of the war into Freddie's mind. Standing that up against the more emotional attitude of Isobel, Freddie began to realise that in viewing the events of the Second World War there were issues concerning individuals, issues concerning communities, issues concerning the military, issues concerning every aspect of life; he said to himself an essay was not going to be enough, Liverpool offered up more than a microcosm of the time. He knew in his heart that this work he was embarking upon was bigger than himself, more important than himself, and relevant to his career.

He lay on his back with the ceiling above him lit from the street light outside and the shadows chasing backwards and forwards above his head seemed like a mystic message to his young mind. It said to him as clearly has anything that the shadows of the past were beginning to show him the shadows of the future.

So surprised at his own almost philosophical thought, Freddie jumped out of bed and got a piece of paper and a pen, and sitting back down at his little table he began to write.

'I am the product of the past, within me I carry all that I have learnt from those who have lived through the past, now I must prepare myself to be what the future needs in order that the world may live at peace. I have only one ambition, I will always fight for peace.'

Returning to his bed, it was another half hour before he fell asleep.

Naturally he overslept, he missed breakfast, and the old couple downstairs, munching on their toast, let him sleep on.

'Did he have a good time last night?' asked Isobel, of her brother.

'I think so; he certainly has some facts to chew upon,' replied Gareth.

Freddie arrived downstairs in time for a cup of coffee at 11.

Chapter 11

The strange day when Freddie understood the need to commit himself to a life of peace.

Gareth Houghton gave voice to the suggestion that all three of them should get in the car and go on a tour to show Freddie some of the different sites that commemorate the damage done to Liverpool during the war.

An hour later they were standing on the corner of Standish Street with Lace Street and reading the account of the bombing raid that wiped out 125 people with one bomb. Known as the Holy Cross Memorial it is now surrounded by new buildings, peaceful looking homes, and in the distance can be seen the Radio City tower formerly known as St John's Tower.

The Pieta statue that is the centrepiece of the memorial was from the Holy Cross Church. Freddie surprised himself by the feelings that were being engendered within him as he looked about the memorial garden. He noticed that both his Aunt and Uncle stood reverently in front of the memorial, their heads bowed; he knew they were praying for all those who had suffered during the war. He was convinced that was what they were doing, something goaded him to go and stand silently beside them; and he even found himself saying a prayer that he had learnt from his mother as a child. He took a breath, a deep breath and thought how is it possible that I can remember being taught those few simple words, 'Eternal rest give unto them, Oh Lord, and let perpetual light shine upon them and may they rest in peace.' He paused, and then said 'Amen.'

The thought came to him, 'How can I carry a memory for so long, of words said at a funeral 15 years previously?' He could not move; he felt himself drawing in his breath, holding it for a second and then letting it out long and slow. Gareth seemed to know that something was bothering the boy, and he reached out and put an arm across Freddie's shoulders saying, 'It's very moving isn't it?'

As Freddie looked up into the eyes of his Uncle something passed between them which said it was all right for a man to have feelings about the death of people he didn't know personally.

'So many of them, it's like an affront to all that's right and proper, I mean they weren't actually fighting were they?' said the young man.

'Do you know about Dresden?' said Isobel.

'Dresden?'

'Yes Dresden, the trouble with war, Freddie, is that they bomb us and we bomb them and people who don't deserve to be killed get in the way. Bombs do what they will do and people die, and it is called collateral damage. But it is about people like you and me and your Uncle Jack.'

There was a strange expression on Isobel's face, turning to look at her Great-nephew she said,

'Look at the news, watch what's going on in the world, and tell me the innocent one doesn't suffer. Freddie, look back over the last 100 years, and tell me that's not true, if you dare?'

'What do you mean, Auntie?'

'Well, think about it Freddie, the First World War, the Second World War, Korea, Belize, Bosnia, Northern Ireland, the Falklands, Iraq and Afghanistan, and all the skirmishes and conflicts masterminded by evil men such as Idi Amin, Gaddafi, Stalin, Putin, you name them, you know them, you are studying modern history, why bother if you think it doesn't matter what happens to the innocent. War, kills off the women and children, the old and infirm, they are unimportant in the minds of evil men.'

'But sometimes Auntie, the soldier fighting these evil men is bound to cause death and destruction. I mean it's always going to happen because, unless you can define the size and shape of the battlefield.'

'Back to Agincourt and Waterloo, eh, Freddie?'

'Yes, I think that's what I mean, I mean nowadays if you have a battle it's in towns and cities and it comes from the air, as well as from cannons that can fire from more than a mile away. How can people escape? And the politicians know that, and the generals, they must know!' queried the younger man.

'Sure they do, it makes for a very nasty equation for the generals, who have to do the bidding of the politicians.'

'Where does the buck stop?' queried Isobel of her great nephew.

They all fell silent, and once more turned back to look at the memorial. As if loathed to break the silence, they quietly turned and walked back towards Cross Hall Street and on towards the shopping centre known as Liverpool One. They walked on until they stood near the Mersey Ferry terminal at the Pier Head, beside the memorial to Captain Johnny Walker, a group commander who escorted convoy after convoy across the Atlantic. Looking about Freddie saw several other memorials and under his breath he said, 'so many, so many!'

They read the inscriptions for the dead of the Merchant Navy, one for the engineers on the Titanic, and other inscriptions some in stone, some in bronze. Walking on they came into the inner walkway of the Albert Dock. A cup of coffee and croissant in the cafe bar of the Tate came next.

'And all this was built by prisoners during the Napoleonic wars: another side-line that pops up during conflicts; free labour, concentration camps. Did you know that the British developed the idea of the camps during the Boer War of 1900?'

Isobel seemed strangely absorbed in her own thoughts until Freddie asked her, 'a penny for them' and once again she took control of the conversation.

'We all have our favourite heroes, my favourite a medical man. Noel Godfrey Chavasse VC and Bar. You must have passed his memorial almost daily walking through Abercromby Square. What a man; we should go up there next.'

Gareth nodded in approval, but added that he wanted to show me other memorials, smaller, less obvious ones.

'Oh, where?' Queried Isobel.

'For a start, few people notice the memorial on platform one at Lime Street station, and what about Blackstock Gardens?'

'True, true and as you said, a walk around St John's Gardens might prove useful,' she added with a solemn face before almost whispering, 'so many, so many!'

We walked back to the car; it was obvious that Isobel was tiring, ever mindful of his sister's health, Gareth called a halt to the outing, 'time for home' he said.

The very compactness of Liverpool city centre and it ready supply of Black Cabs meant that we were able to get from the Albert Dock to our car parked back at Standish Street in a matter of minutes.

'Had a good day, young man?' asked Gareth.

I smiled, nodded my head, and realising that we were all relaxing in the taxicab that it was probably time to apologise for my tardiness that morning.

'I'm sorry I was late this morning,'

'No problem young Freddie, it's no matter? Did the drink knock you out?'

Within minutes they were once again in front of the Holy Cross memorial, and Freddie stood looking at the Picta, in silence, until his emotional reaction to the morning's events came bursting out.

"Well, it was Bert's fault, I just had to look up some of the things he'd said, to see if they were really true; and the awful truth is, they were true! There were pictures of an overhead railway that has been bomb near James Street, and I thought that didn't look too bad, but somehow the more I looked at it the more it became real, the way it was hanging in mid-air and people standing around looking at it, but, it didn't say anything about a hundred and twenty five people sheltering in a school-basement next door to a church, I mean just as with the bomb that fell on this street, so there was another article about 365 people being killed on the 20th to 22nd of December 1940. Yes, 365 killed just days before Christmas, and it is calmly written up as the 'Christmas blitz of 1940' like a fairy story, like it felt remote, like it was nothing. I mean that there were accounts of places, really important places, like the Customs House, like the Bluecoat Chambers and other places, all of them bombed at different times, and according to the article, Liverpool suffered the most after London, but you'd never know it, today nobody remembers, it's all said so matter-of-factly, why isn't everyone screaming about it? You and I do remember Coventry, we have all heard of that, it's always in the news, whenever they want to talk about bombing and civilians dying they talk about Coventry, but has anybody anywhere ever heard of the bombing of Liverpool?"

Gareth smiled at Freddie before putting a gentle hand on his shoulder and saying,

"For Coventry it all happened on one night, the bombing of Liverpool was kept quiet because nobody wanted Hitler and his cronies to know if they had been successful in cutting of our supplies."

"You mean Liverpool was more important than Coventry?"

"In a way, yes, I suppose that's exactly what I'm saying. The docks were our life line."

"Sorry Uncle I didn't mean to sound angry, but after reading all that stuff on the Web, I felt ashamed, and last night I made a promise to myself. Shall I tell you?'

'Only if you want to Freddie.' said Isobel.

'I vowed that if I was allowed only one ambition, it would be that I will always fight for peace, no matter what my future life may be.'

Freddie was so obviously physically and emotionally moved by what he had just said that both his Aunt and Uncle moved closer to him; the three of them stood with their arms around each other, in silence and trust. The moment embedded itself in Freddie's emotions and would live there for the rest of his life; mirroring the Pieta and silently telling him that he must realize that he would suffer for his vow.

'Am I strong enough?' He voiced and in silence the others simply hugged him closer as if they realised what the boy was feeling at that moment.

It was Isobel who asked Gareth to take us to Blackstock Gardens. How can I write of my feelings as I stood as respectfully as I could before the memorial to over two hundred civilians killed by one bomb on the 21st of December 1940?

I repeated my vow.

Chapter 12

Memories of VE day and VJ Day

By the time we had returned to the house it was nearly 4 o'clock, the autumn sun had disappeared behind grey clouds and the three of us settled in the front sitting room with tea and crumpets, 'To keep us going,' was Gareth's comment.

It was Isobel who moved my thoughts away from what we had seen that day on to happier times.

'I suppose my happiest memory was of VE day. It was like magic.'

'Oh, Auntie, let me get my tape recorder, I don't want to miss anything.'

Gareth returned to the kitchen, saying, 'I think I'll cook us a special meal, we've had a tiring day. You learn about the parties and I'll go and cook. I've heard it all before.'

Laughing, I asked him if he was suggesting that his sister was boring, to which he replied, 'No, but as I said I've heard it all before.'

'Don't mind him,' said Isobel, 'he really does want to get on with the evening meal. It will be a

proper meal because we've only been nibbling all day. You can't stop him cooking; I always laugh at him and say he should be on the telly. They have enough stupid cooks on TV who can't cook anywhere near as well as he does. And have you noticed the way he flips that knife around? My goodness nobody cuts vegetables up the way he does. Everything is lined up like soldiers, all the carrots à la Julienne, all the celery, all the peppers, all the potatoes come out from under his whirling Sabatier's and whatever he is doing, it's all lined up like a regiment in front of him and only then does he start cooking the meal. It's his craft and he loves it; but I suspect he misses his sous chefs.'

'He likes his dishwasher, I know, because when I offered to wash up, he said, 'No worry, why do you think I've got a dishwasher?' I had laughed at that and told him I wanted it because one dish washer was not enough for my student digs. Well, then he laughed back at me saying, 'Over my dead body!', So, I know he thinks his dishwasher is an important part of his life.'

Isobel and I laughed heartily before she made a gesture at the tape recorder, 'Let's get on with it, lad.'

Somehow or other Isobel seemed alive as she spoke of V E day. Apparently, her mother had found an old blue dress that fitted Isobel, and together they had sewn on red and white ribbon. Everybody was singing and laughing as dining tables and kitchen tables were carried out into the centre of the road to create an enormously long table.

"This was covered with different sheets and tablecloths and adorned with plates of fish paste sandwiches, of spam sandwiches, and I think there were some lettuce sandwiches, sneaked from someone's greenhouse."

At that I interrupted her with, "Lettuce sandwiches?"

Isobel laughed at my query, "Oh, Freddie you've not lived if you've never had lettuce sandwiches. Fresh baked Bloomer bread, now we have them with butter, but then it was with margarine, a lettuce leaf or two, sprinkled with malt vinegar and caster sugar. A sweet and sour sandwich! Of cause then the sugar was very sparing and sometimes it was more vinegar sour than sugar sweet." Isobel laughed as she then said, "You should try them!"

"Yuk, no thanks, Auntie," I said, but she was enjoying my discomfort as she carried on with her description of VE day.

"Then somehow or other there was jelly and fruit, well not a lot of fruit, but I remember some cherries in the jelly. Mother made some small cakes and then cut the tops off and cutting the tops in half she created fairy wings to stand up with the aid of some butter icing, made with margarine and she named them Fairy Cakes. It all looked magical, we were unbelievably happy, and the mantra heard time and time again, was 'Daddy will soon be home.' Every child in the street was saying it, every mother was laughing.

Later that night a bonfire was lit in a nearby park and we were all given a potato to put in the embers to cook and to eat as the evening of song and dance continued way past our bedtime. I'm always surprised that the potatoes were the only real memory your Great Uncle Eddie lays claim to, so I can never talk with him about that time in his life.

Going home was a bit of a disappointment, poor old South Essex had taken a severe battering, but we survived and I remember the VJ party was a much more subdued event compared with the VE party, but look, here is a photo of the VJ party, and there I am, and that's your Great Aunt Rosie. It was lovely to be back with her, and I went to school, this time to find that I was behind with my learning, especially my spelling.

It was a strange time, like that eerie time before a storm: until just before Christmas 1945, when Daddy came home."

I thought that would be it: that she would have nothing more to say, but I was wrong, there was so much still causing her distress.

Great Aunt Isobel shifted herself in her chair until she was comfortable, and then she said something I will never forget,

"This stranger came home; it was not the smiling man who had rescued me from the hospital, when I was lost, no! It was a violent, angry, almost vicious man who walked through the door late that night. I could see him through the door of the bedroom; remember we were all sleeplng ln the same bedroom on the ground floor!"

I nodded; she seemed pleased that I had remembered that fact. Isobel seemed smaller than usual, almost as if she was cowering, as she faced up to what she felt she had to tell me.

"Do you want to stop, Auntie?" I asked quietly. She shook her head, but her face was solemn as she continued.

"I was excited, so excited that as I stood up to run to him, with my arms lifted up in happiness, I wet myself. I couldn't help it. I stood there in a puddle of my own wee as his face became enraged and he turned me over and slapped my bottom, almost screaming at me, calling me a filthy whore. He must have hit me a dozen times, I was sore for days after. Mummy had tried to stop him and he lashed out at her. The noise was horrendous. I was crying, Mummy was crying and he just stood there seething with anger, calling Mummy all sorts of names, accusing her of being a bad mother, he even shouted at her because it was only the second time he actually saw Gareth. Gareth takes after Mother's side of the family: as a ten month old baby he had blonde curly hair and bright blue eyes, the only one of us to have such a fair haired look, at that age.

Christmas was a strange time, he shouted one minute and the next he seemed morose. Large as the rooms were, it nevertheless seemed as it the whole place was too small for the seven of us. The council intervened and found a three-bedded house half a mile away.

Within a year of the war, we were moved. With more space we all hoped for a better home life, but no, his violence continued. It was bad enough being poor, cold and living in a damp bomb damaged house, without having to watch Mummy being treated so badly. I think she took it because she was afraid of him hitting her children. There were nights when he locked her out of the house. Yes, he forced her out onto the street, I seem to remember his shouting that she could go back to her mother if she wanted to, he didn't care, as he slammed and locked the door.

But Charlie soon sorted things out. Before we went up to bed Charlie made certain that the key was in the door of the front parlour, and the door was locked. He had noticed that Daddy had a habit of checking all the doors and windows every night; that is except the front parlour, there he only rattled the door handle. It was customary not to use that room except for entertaining visitors:

Charlie and I would wait until we heard Daddy come up to bed, then Charlie would listen for his snoring. When we were certain it was safe, we would wave to Mummy from my bedroom window, indicating an 'all clear' and she would open the parlour's sash window and climb in to sleep on the sofa. Then the next morning when a satisfied and silent daddy left for work, we would unlock the parlour door and let Mummy out. Years later daddy spoke of believing she had gone to her mother's house. The secret of our success lay in the amazing artistic talent of Charlie: he created a false looking window catch, which hid the open catch, a precaution in case Daddy should change his usual pattern and looked into the room. There must have been at least twelve occasions when Mummy was locked out by a tormented nearly crazy man: but it all added to the years of hating him that I carried with me, like a painful stone buried in my heart. Looking back I believe that I was also angry because he did nothing in the mornings to help me get the children up and ready for school: he just shouted at me to get on with it. By the time I was seven I was completely domesticated and able to mind all the children.

When he had left for work, we let Mummy out of the front parlour. She would smile and kiss us and say, "He can't help it, it was the war!" Charlie and I would vent our hate, but she would say, "He was a lovely man before the war, so handsome, so kind. One day he will be better."

And my beautiful mother endured those five or six years of his violent temper, his heavy-handed slapping, his thoughtless spending of his wages, of mounting debts, of two more pregnancies, which left her even more worn out and distressed, before we were at last moved, shortly before Christmas 1953, into a newly built four bedroomed home. "Do you know Freddie; it was Gareth who sorted Daddy out. About 1955, he got him to the doctors where after blood tests and drugs and injections, we found out that he had been left both physically and mentally ill, by all that had happened to him during the last two years of the war. Poor man, but back then, I still found it hard to forgive him."

There was a pause that seemed somehow different, almost unrehearsed as she said, .

"It was years later watching Patrick Stewart on one of those, 'Who do you think you are?'

programmes that I fully realized that daddy could not have been fully responsible for his behaviour. Then I began to forgive him, it was such a relief to know that it wasn't my fault that he was ill. Mummy was right, it was the War! It was labelled shell shock and he still could not speak of it, but as treatment progressed and he got less tired, some level of peace came to all of us. I can't pretend that he was cured of his bad temper over night, he was still fragile, but twelve years after the war, the war ended for Mummy and us children.

Chapter 13

Rebuilding Isobel's world.

"The house helped: it was one of the first newly constructed council houses. You may well ask why it took so long to rebuild our town, our country.

Freddie, there was a shortage of building materials, as well as a shortage of food. People were angry and yet we knew that we had to feed half of Europe, and rebuild places like Dresden, and other places we had bombed.

Hard was it was, Mummy coped, she was amazing, I still remember her seventeen recipes, for feeding her family of nine, with just a four ounce tin of Corned Beef as the daily protein. Imagine, for seven children and two adults the choice was, corned beef hash, or corned beef fritters, or corned beef croquettes, oh dear, I can't bore you with the whole list, but she was amazing. Two pounds of potatoes, skins on mind you, boiled and mashed with the corned beef and any other root vegetables she had to hand, before being shaped and rolled in homemade breadcrumbs and deep fried!

I never forget that deep fat frying pan. Every bit of dripping from fried mince, from sausages, and other occasional bits of suet were all added to the pan. It gave an extraordinary flavour to everything. Sometimes I have gone past a café, the type that we would call a 'Greasy Joe's' and I am reminded of the all-pervasive smell of our post-war kitchen.

My brothers were always hungry, not even school dinners could satisfy them. And as for Daddy, he was given the family bacon ration more often than not for his Sunday breakfast, or his evening meal. Oh dear, breakfast! For years our only choice was 'bread porridge' cubes of stale bread, stewed in milk and sweetened with Black Molasses. Yuk!"

"Auntie, how awful!" was all I could think to say, until she suddenly leant forward and with a wicked grin and giving a giggle that was surprising in its sweetness, she added, "It was magic if the truth be told, especially during the forties when we had no toothpaste and had to clean our teeth with a mixture of soot and salt. Oh dear, am I repeating myself? Didn't I tell you about the soot a while ago?"

"Don't worry Auntie just keep repeating yourself, I love listening to you."

"If you're humouring me, I'll smack you!"

At that I gave a yell that Gareth heard in the kitchen. He came running in with an anxious look on his face. Seeing Isobel roaring with laughter and me almost bent double in disgust at the idea of cleaning teeth with soot from the chimney mixed with salt, he smiled and after I explained my reaction, he added the information that people mostly cleaned their teeth with tooth power of one sort or another. Paste was a luxury we knew nothing about until well into the fifties.

"Dinner in ten minutes," was his final comment.

That night I researched more and more about how people coped with rationing. I had Googled the question: "Exactly how much food was allocated to each person by the rationing books," I found a picture of both the food and clothing books and a faded petrol coupon for one unit of petrol.

Ration books were like lifelines that your mother guarded carefully. Lost or stolen books created huge problems for people. Mostly the weekly ration was for just two ounces of tea, the same weight of two ounces each of cheese, butter, margarine, bacon, lard, and sugar. Porridge, shredded wheat or wheat flakes were available on some occasions. Fortunately root vegetables could be home grown, and several people apparently grew a lot of their own. Gardens and allotments were highly prized spaces, religiously planted with seasonal food crops; not a square inch was wasted.

All the accounts spoke of the wonderful support given during the first two years of the war by Canada: it is universally agreed that Great Britain would have starved to death without their wonderful generosity in shipping basic foodstuffs across the Atlantic. Again I saw a strong link to Liverpool being mentioned. As to the reluctance of the USA during the early days of the War, to send supplies across the Atlantic, well it was not until after Pearl harbour that America gradually came on board to add to the work already being done by Canada.

I felt myself questioning other aspects of Home Front life. What were the issues concerning transport and petrol? Petrol was only allowed for military or for work related tasks. Interesting, when you look at some film and TV dramas, you never find an image of petrol coupons being traded on the black market, and who today has heard that there was a thirty mile limit upon movements by the non-military population? So, how could those romantics trips into the countryside have happened? Eat your heart out Hollywood; I was beginning to see some flaws in some of your productions.

It was late, I was tired, but my head was spinning with a realisation that history can be twisted by writers, by media, by just a few words or actions misrepresenting the truth. I was *beginning to appreciate the feeling of truth as being an essential ingredient in the telling of history. Sometimes the ugliness of the truth is lost in the telling, as the author tries to make the work 'commercial or box office perfect' to increase sales, but as I listened again to the last tape; I just knew I was hearing the truth. I can still hear Isobel telling me, "Swallows and Amazons are all very well, but for many children, war is a nightmare that stays with them for the rest of their lives." She had spoken the truth; she still remembered every detail. And every detail still hurt her. No written account could have conveyed such feelings: at last I understood the wisdom of my tutor, Mr Edward Greenfield.*

Chapter 14

Freddie's Dad is pleased at last.

The week was over, I was due back at Uni, and I felt a loss that I could never have believed possible. But it's true, I missed the gentle warmth of that old couple, and deep down inside myself I recognized that I was changed by all that I had seen and heard.

My fellow students later said that they had noticed a change in me.

For a start I had become interested in the news, in reports of wars still raging around the world. I took more responsibility for the mess I made at our digs, a fact upon which the girls complemented me. The truly fascinating thing is that I was the one who did not initially notice the change.

The puzzle was solved when I returned home for Christmas, to find Aunt Isobel and Uncle Gareth sitting in front of our home fire.

"I invited them as a way of thanking them for helping you," declared my mother.

A week later, Gareth drove them both back to Liverpool. I missed them almost immediately, but it was Father who said at dinner, that night, "I can see how much you admire Gareth, good; very good!"

I looked at him in bewilderment.

"You are copying his mannerisms; you have taken note of his more military attitudes. It's all good. No more untidy rooms, at table on time and even helping in the kitchen. Very good!"

Poor old Dad, he hasn't changed, but I struck while the iron of communication was red hot and asked,

"Dad, do you remember your own Grandfather?"

By the time he had finished I knew how and what and why I was to become the man who would record the history culled from the living, before it was lost, to leave it to future generations, so that they may learn from both the mistakes and the triumphs of the past, as they build the future for the good of all mankind. Most of all I was to become angered by the abundance of hurt dished out to children, as the greed of mankind fought for territory, for political or religious supremacy.

I now saw history as a baton passing from one generation to the next and promised myself that I would strive to abide by the truthfulness I had witnessed in Great Aunt Isobel, in my writings, both as a journalist and as an historian.

Somewhere along the line, I had come to appreciate that teaching was not for me, I needed to spread my talents for the benefit of all children.

Chapter 15

<u>Freddie gets a job.</u>

Three years later, with a modest 2-2 degree under my belt, and with financial help from my father, I indulged in a post-graduation gap year working for the Red Cross, and eventually, with thanks to a sizeable amount of family led nepotism, I ended up working in Sierra Leone, as a roving reporter for a British Red Top. They had approved of my efforts to highlight the personal stories around the nurses and doctors fighting the epidemic. I believed that with the Ebola crisis developing at that time, fear kept the bigger names away, I was expendable, and who would miss me if I died of Ebola? Thus they offered me a stipend to enable me to carry on for the best part of another nine months.

I told the story with as much truthfulness as I could and felt a degree of pride in my achievements, when seeing more and more of my by-lines being published almost verbatim, I was increasingly satisfied with my attempts to record actual living history, for there was no denying I had a sense of history in the making, as I reported on the dreadful problems that surrounded that epidemic. If I had achieved anything of note to impress my editors, it was that I found myself focusing upon the stories of the hundreds of orphans, lost to the public gaze as seemingly more important issues swallowed up official attention. I began to feel that headlines always concentrated upon the money matters, ahead of the needs or the importance of the children. I found myself thinking of Isobel's accounts of being evacuated and compared them to my witnessing of the poverty of these orphans. There was no worthy comparison; the very climate was brutal in its intensity. I watched half-starved toddlers lying in the very dirt, covered with sweat and being plagued by flies, as they waited for help to come. So many times help did not come. So many died.

There came a day when it was over 40°Centigrade and I found it unbearable as sweat poured down my body, from under my hair, over my face and drenching every centimetre of my aching flesh. I thought of the plastic sheeting worn as protection by the staff trying to deal with the epidemic. "Dear God, help the doctors and nurses garbed up against the threat of Ebola!" Well, I never was a great prayer-man: but my heart was reaching out for those striving to heal the sick, while their protective clothes added to their own suffering. I felt helpless and useless as I watched at a reasonably safe distance. As prayers go it was nothing, but it must have got through because suddenly my editor felt I needed to travel to Kenya, and report on a terrorist attack which had occurred the day before. It was urgent and I felt exhilarated again, until some shame began registering in my mind: I was gratefully boarding an air conditioned plane to fly to Kenya. I was young and fit and I felt I was walking away like a coward afraid of an unseen but devastating disease, whereas in Kenya, just because it was a terrorist attack, I could hopefully see the enemy and avoid it.

A university had been attacked by a terrorist group: students had been needlessly killed by a violent gang calling themselves Boko Haram. This time I was able to make contact with a survivor, and highlighted her story. Suddenly my bi-line was a global commodity, but I simply felt I was reaping the benefit of old Edward Greenfield's policy of speaking to the living whenever, wherever, you find them.

I found a young girl who had already endured several serious traumas as a young child. Losing both her parents to the Aids virus, Chriki found herself taken in by an Aunt, who died six months later, and then by her elderly grandmother, who too old and sick to work sent her eight year old granddaughter to work in a neighbour's field. It was subsistence living, but she survived. Then at ten years of age, a miracle happened and an educational Charity called The Mango Tree Trust discovered her and Chriki's life was transformed. Education followed and she had managed to study and eventually get to university where she had been learning to be a doctor. The horror of the attack that she had endured at the hands of the Boko Haran was still evident in the trembling of her tiny body, in the silent tears streaming down her cheeks and in the wringing of her hands, as if trying to wipe away the blood of her best friend. Chriki owed her life to her friend who having been shot had fallen taking Chriki with her and thus protecting Chriki from the bullets being sprayed around the lecture hall. She had lain as if dead, beneath her friend, to save her own life. I remembered Great Aunt Isobel and her account of seeing her mother injured, and I knew that for this wee soul, no matter how successful her life might be, the nightmare she had survived was to be with her forever.

But I had no time to stay and follow up on her story, within days I was posted to Egypt where political trials were already in progress, and I thought great, settle down; this will be a long bloodless stay trying to gain access to court rooms. No such luck, two days later, against British Consulate advice, I was sent along the North African coast to do a story about a boat load of migrants drowning in the Mediterranean Sea. Promised a cameraman of some experience to accompany me on this assignment, I felt I had at last arrived as a serious journalist. The journey into Libya was an extraordinary experience, but I suddenly felt a degree of success was coming my way: I was no longer a solo journalist who had to snap his own supporting pictures, I had a burly, but friendly professional cameraman named Norman, older and wiser, who became a wonderful free educator for this still rookie journalist.

Years later I was to learn that Norman Probert had offered his services to my boss, on the strength of my earliest work in Sierra Leone.

"You focus on the people," was his explanation for turning up at my hotel in Tripoli.

I had chosen the Awal Hotel because I needed some comfort in the heat. I had been in Africa for six months and I just wanted a rest from the relentless heat: oh, judge me if you will, but I was still an Englishman underneath all the bravado of slumming it at Uni, who liked his comfort when he could get it. Was I not a spoilt only child from a home run by reasonably wealthy professional parents?

Norman Probert welcomed my choice of hotel. We shared a twin bedded room, it seemed economically a more sound investment and it gave us the opportunity to discuss our work plans in private.

"Ok, Fred," he said the next morning almost immediately we woke that first morning, *"So we are going after the trafficking bastards?"*

"That's my intention," I said, *"but where to begin: any ideas?"*

"Well, this is going to take a few days; my suggestion might be, let's just walk around as

tourists today, lazy like, know what I mean? I'll take my Canon with me, it looks more of a tourist camera than my others, yes, we can leave the rest of this stuff locked up, and if I see anything useful I can just snap it, it won't look as if we are snooping, if we don't get too close."

"You've done this before?"

"Yes, but I don't consider myself paparazzi, Oh no, just more 'curious with courtesy' is my motto."

I laughed out loud; I liked that, 'Curious with courtesy!' He smiled back at me, I felt reassured by his humour and his relaxed approach as we headed off for a buffet style breakfast in the air conditioned dining room. The Awal was not a massive tower block of a hotel, it had a more intimate feel to it and its external features could be labelled as modest, to the point that it seemed like a place that didn't wish to attract attention. But its four stars rating seemed justified on our initial experience of the place.

No more than half an hour after breakfast and there we were, a casually sauntering pair of tourists watching the activity along the beach, and smiling at all and sundry with a curiosity synonymous with newbie visitors to the region. Norman was hilarious; he had a way with him that made people laugh back. Walking with his head held high as if looking at birds or planes, he endlessly collided with the general population in such a manner that he had to apologise, and thereby he nearly always managed to develop a conversation which, after half a dozen encounters, gave us more information that I could ever have hoped for on our first day.

By lunchtime we were sitting on cushions placed upon carpets, in a dirty noisy makeshift place, drinking coffee. I cannot call it a café or even an outside kitchen to a home. It was simply a dirt floor space between two fairly large commercial premises. If England has a surfeit of John Smiths and Wales has its multiple examples of Dai Jones; Libya has a surfeit of Ali's, Hassam's or Khaled's. But Norman took it all without any annoyance, he just chatted away using odd words and many hand gestures, with a rather sweet faced girl who said her name was Fatima and an hour later, after a quick visit to our hotel to pay up and to collect our proper luggage, we were heading out of the centre of Tripoli to beyond the concreted walkway favoured by tourists, to a more deserted part of the coast. Yes, we were driving our hired car and I had been handed an enormous map to hold.

"Now remember, Fred, we are tourists and tourists get lost, we get near anything interesting, look as if you are trying to find something on that and don't look at those looking at us. I'll do that, my face can gurney any emotion, so accept that I will loudly and rudely blame you for our being lost! Comprendre?"

"Don't tell me you're bi-lingual and a former actor who has studied human nature! You remind me of my cousin Frankie, I never know who or what he is, he calls it acting, and I call it deception. He once turned up at our house dressed as an insurance salesman and none of us recognised him. It was hilarious."

"Right, so you know what I want from you: we have to get this end of the story; who are the traffickers? It's what the papers want."

"It's what everyone wants," I said quietly as he drove on and on, only slowing down when he saw a group of people sitting along the road side as if waiting for something to happen.

"They look as if they have been dumped," Norman observed and I felt obliged to agree with him. He stopped the car and started shouting at me, pointing at the map, as if I was to blame for his problem.

"You stupid idiot, this is all wrong, can't you do as asked, where is Tripoli? Show me, where is Tripoli?"

He jumped out of the car and strutted around waving his arms about in frustration and them he stood in front of a group of men pleading, "Tripoli? Tripoli?"

It worked: a young alert looking twenty something boy of a man, came forward and speaking in English, said, "Sir, you go that way."

I never heard the rest, Norman shook hands with the young man and turned on me with a shaking of a fist and his face contorted in a ferocious anger and I performed a suitable contrite pose. Back he turned to his new friend, Muhammad something; I did not catch his name. I just stood there by the car watching the two of them examining the map. Again I marvelled at Norman Probert engineering the younger man towards a rock upon which they could sit as they explore various routes to places of interest. Well, that was what it looked like.

They talked for over an hour; I fanned myself in the heat, sitting in the dust, my back against the side of the car, as I watched both Norman and the silent mass of people gathered just metres from me. Fear crept into me mind as I looked at their exhausted faces. What were they waiting for, possibly a bus, but more likely a boat.

Eventually Norman came back and hurled himself into the driver's seat as I climbed stiffly into the oven that was the hired car. "He is from Eritrea," was all Norman said.

He turned the car around and drove about half a kilometre back towards Tripoli. Then stopping in the shadow from off a whitewashed wall, he switched off the engine and said. "Shut your eyes; look as if you are asleep."

I tried to relax, tried to look detached from Norman, rather in the manner and style of the youthful indifference I had shown my Father, on so many occasions. Norman woke me by pulling at my arm, "Don't say a word." I understood the sound of authority in his voice and opening my eyes behind my Polaroid's: I witnessed a dilapidated single decker coach driving past, full of Africans of every colour and age. The noise of the engine spoke of age and overload.

Glancing at Norman I remained silent as he started the engine and followed the coach at a hopefully safe distance. We drove past the area where we had originally met up with the young man from Eritrea. There was no sign of any of them, just a few sweet wrappers, probably discarded by children, to ever show that humans had gathered in that spot. Norman stopped the car and in the silence we waited. The heat was unbearable we were cooking in the oven that was our hired Europcar. It was French and comfortable enough, when we were moving with windows open and the fans whirring. Static and aware that we were miles from a garage, Norman opted against sitting with the air-conditioning eating up the battery. Adding, "It is like sitting in a fan assisted oven, you cook regardless! Get used to it, just keep drinking and take this." He handed me a small teabag sized sachet of white powder.

"Salt and sugar, keeps you hydrated!"

I obeyed and poured its contents into the remains of my bottle of Evian water. I watched it troth up in a million bubbles and hurriedly put the bottle to my mouth to catch the precious liquid. It was the first of many survival tricks I was to learn from Norman.

Norman heard an engine starting about a mile ahead, suddenly, he started the ignition and we burst forward as if chasing an unseen prey. For about 20 miles we followed at a reasonably safe distance the coach we had seen earlier.

We came to an area that had once been a vibrant and walled property: today it was in ruins and yet they were sufficient to hide hundreds of the gathering migrants. Norman hid the car away from the road behind a sand dune.

Together we crept forward keeping ourselves hid behind the undulating coastal dunes until we had full sight of the migrants being loaded onto different boats. Some were inflatables, and a couple were incredibly ancient looking fishing vessels. Norman snapped pictures of everything he believed was important: most notably as many faces of the controllers as he could: and in particular of one very elegant looking middle-aged man.

Norman said to me, "if I didn't know better, I'd believe he was a lawyer, he looks like a fat illegitimate bastard to me."

We waited in silence until realising that the organisers were returning to their coach, we raced back to our car, in readiness to follow them. It was a difficult journey we had to somehow or other kept sufficient distance from the coach, but with the use of some binoculars, which I had sensibly brought with me; I had noted the licence plate of the bus and of a jeep that had mysteriously appeared from within the compound.

We journeyed west, further away from Tripoli, and I was getting worried that we would run out of petrol. But I needn't have worried, we skirted around bend after bend as we descended down a steep twisting road, until we found ourselves looking down upon the town of Nulat.

"Don't worry kid," Norman said, "I know just the place for a drink and a cool off. Then if you will take my advice I suggest we contact our own authorities with the information that we have, you are okay about that?"

I couldn't have been happier, my mind and my heart felt sentiments were hurting me more than I could possibly have anticipated. There is more than a sense of helplessness that caring people feel when confronted with the cruelty inflicted upon others, by greedy and powerful criminals.

Sitting in the shade of a tearoom garden in the centre of the town, I dug out my laptop and was able to connect to the wireless connection available. My report sent to the paper, was followed by as long an email as I could possibly have written, to my darling great-aunt, telling her yet more of my adventures and promising to call in and see her as soon as possible.

Norman meanwhile had gone off and found the police station, where using his usual devious charms he had managed to track the details of the owner of both the bus and the jeep, before returning to join me. After a long discussion we decided not to inform the local authorities of our findings, but to return to Egypt and report to the British.

"We'll head for Cairo and the Garden City. Can't remember the name of the road, but I do know the embassy is in the garden city area. It would be easy enough to find once we get there." said Norman, who was looking at me: as if to say, 'Stop worrying kid!'

Yes, he still treated me as a rookie, but I didn't mind, I knew I had much to learn and I controlled any urge to be cocky about the situation, in which we found ourselves. Stocking up with more petrol, plenty of water, and food sufficient for three days, we set off for Egypt and Cairo. When I queried the amount of food and supplies stacked in the car boot, Norman explained that being prepared was part of his policy when journeying outside towns and cities.

"You will learn kid," he said with a grin on his face and kindness in his voice, "that to survive in foreign lands keep an eye on your own basic needs. Hot country equals plenty of water, cold country means keeping warm, with her knickers if necessary. I've often worn silk underwear that my *wife brought for herself. Amazing, such a thin layer but so successful in keeping me warm. And the other thing I've learnt, don't strip off in the sun, sunburn is a disaster."*

We laughed, we almost cried, as we shared stories of our education and our families. I learned that Norman Probert had come from a large and happy family from the middle of Suffolk.

"Fields to play in, good schooling, and plenty of haystacks by the time I was 15. I'm still married to her, I adore my Susan, and I love that she is a homemaker. Yes, I always return to a loving home, my four kids and a house full of pets."

"And your Susan doesn't mind you travelling like you do?"

"No, I have an agent who looks after me; keeps to my rules, three months on and three months off: always Christmas at home that's number one."

I liked Norman more and more and by the time we had landed back at Heathrow, a week later, I felt I had made a friend for life. That he also expressed a wish that we might work together in the future and different assignments made me feel that I had been reasonably good at my job on this occasion.

Chapter 16

<u>*A Real Home Coming.*</u>

First stop off was to the paper and a very comforting session with the editor, who complimented me on my work. I tried to remain modest and unaffected by what he said, but secretly I was proud that I had succeeded. He particularly congratulated me on how I had compared those elements from history that were being reflected in modern day history. Evidently, he felt that I hadn't been so far off kilter when comparing the social effects of the Black Death to the current repercussions of the Ebola crisis. And he had said that linking the dreadful plight of the dispossessed after the Second World War to the plight of the dispossessed of the 21st-century, I had created some interesting anomalies still existing in the minds of nation leaders, and in truth, the entire population of the so-called First World towards the poor of the Third World, in particular how I seem to have an understanding of the special effects of war, upon women and children. It was sufficient a pat on the back, followed by the promise of future assignments, to give a lift to my step, as I left the office and headed for home.

Then two nights at home; where for once I found my parents willing to listen to my story. My father looked me straight in the eye as he informed me, "Freddie, I felt your reports were very well written. Very insightful and detailed, and I felt proud of you, very proud of you indeed. I'm not sure I could have travelled into those ghastly places, I'm just glad you come home safely."

Driving up north and into Liverpool via the M62, I felt my heart lift with an even greater sense of coming home. What is it about our university Alma Maters? For me, it will always be the place where I found not only myself, and an awakening understanding about life, it was where I had met my wonderful great aunt and uncle. Yes, reader, you have guessed it, I drove straight to their home, and rushed in with my arms full of flowers and chocolates, and a bottle of the best red wine I could afford for dear Gareth.

Again I heard that wonderful phrase, "I'm so proud of you." Coming first from Isobel, and later from Gareth, I knew that I had at long last measured up in the eyes of the two people I personally admired most in the world.

I am no longer a dreamer; thanks to them I faced my future with an understanding that as a journalist, I can look to the past to see some of the patterns for the future. But no matter what, I will always see the children. I will always judge politicians and nations by how they treat women and children, for life begins with them and society is destroyed without them.

Today I work as a roving reporter for UNICEF and UNESCO, following all those principles I learnt from Gareth and Isobel and true to my promise to always work for peace. Luckily Norman is often able to join me, and we extend our recordings to the moving images of film and TV.

Then, when possible, I call upon my relatives and friends to help with fundraising for numerous children's charities. Angela is especially kind giving piano concerts all over the world. In a small way they each promote their different skills to help the children, and in doing so receive a wider recognition of their own talents.

For me, things are very different.

There is nothing I need, for while I am given the strength and grace to serve humanity by being the voice of the many persecuted women and children of the world, I am content.

Every year, I revisit Liverpool and renew my vow, and remember Isobel and Gareth and all they stood for in the silence of their warm and loving home. I visit the memorial at Blackstock Gardens and without embarrassment I lay a bunch of flowers, before making my way to the Pieta at the corner of Standish Street with Lace Street, in the heart of Liverpool. There too I honour the dead with another floral tribute, whispering, "You are not forgotten." Standing there I remember why I pledged to work for peace, for women and children wounded by the traumas caused by megalomaniacs; both religious and political.

In my heart I remember sitting with Gareth in the gardens of St Luke's and I know why I remember the spirit that is Liverpool. It is the people who make the City and in a strange way the chemistry is shared, for the City reciprocates the honour. Liverpool is the city where I always feel at home, at home with its history, at home with its refusal to lay down and die quietly, no matter what is thrown at it.

Last stop, before returning to my busy life, I sit quietly by the memorial stone I had placed in the Springwood Cemetery to my greatest teachers, Isobel and Gareth. I hear them still, for while I live, they will never be forgotten.

11619662R00119

Printed in Great Britain
by Amazon.co.uk, Ltd.,
Marston Gate.